Still Pushing Pineapples

In early April 2021 I received a call from a mutual friend asking me if I was prepared to be interviewed by Dene on his superb Sunday radio show on True Radio (the home of proper good music) to talk about my experiences in forty years of retailing and hosting celebrity book events.

Following the three part interview Dene invited me into his Organisation to help produce, edit, market and promote this book and to liaise with his publisher. I agreed without hesitation.

Although I knew Dene as the "Agadoo" and Black Lace man, it has only been whilst working with him that I have realised that not only is he hugely talented, but he is also a genuinely lovely guy.

It has been both a pleasure and a privilege to work with Dene and his team in helping create and manage this project.

I hope you enjoy reading Dene's truly fascinating story.

David Shapiro
Dene Michael Organisation
July 22nd 2021

Publisher	5T Publishing Nemus House, 32 London Rd, Stockport, Cheshire SK7 4AH UK Email: info@5Tpublishing.com Tel: 0161 482 7800	All rights reserved	No part of this publication may be reproduced in any form or by any means, electronic, mechanical, photocopying, recording or otherwise without the prior written consent of the publisher or Dene Michael.
Copyright	©Dene Michael Betteridge		
Design & Art Direction	Steve Collins	'Still Pushing Pineapples'	Dene Michael asserts his moral and legal right to be identified as the author of this work.
Artwork	Mark Goodwin		
First published	2021		
Reprint	10 9 8 7 6 5 4 3 2 1 0	First Printed in Great Britain by Galloways for 5T Publishing	2021
ISBN	978-1-9161900-2-3		
A catalogue record of this book is available from the British Library		Designed and produced by 5T Publishing All rights reserved.	

5 PUBLISHING

This book is dedicated to
my Mum and Dad
and my 4 wonderful children
and 10 grandchildren
and of course my brother Simon
and my 2 nephews.

Contents

Dene Michael

Foreword

David King

When I was approached to write this foreword, it took no time at all for me to agree to write it. Dene Michael is not only a hugely talented artiste, but he is also a generous man who will go out of his way to help people, wherever he can. Dene's ability on stage is legendary, and his legions of fans who stretch halfway round the world, simply adore him.

I was introduced to Dene many years ago by music producer Lawrence Stone. He came to see me with an idea for a touring show and he brought Dene along to meet me. I was instantly impressed with his warmth and charisma. I had seen him on stage and admired his superb performance and the way he had the audience eating out of the palms of his hands.

I have produced many shows over the years, including my hit Irish dance show Spirit of the Dance. I have been fortunate to have worked with the great and good of showbusiness, including Sir Elton John, Lionel Richie, Sir Rod Stewart and many more. In my opinion, Dene Michael is in good company with these music greats.

I am sure you will enjoy this book. It will give you, the reader, a secret look into the world of showbusiness through Dene's eyes.

It is a warts n' all reflection of a fascinating career, a turbulent personal life, and most importantly, a captivating, behind the scenes look at the life and times of my good friend, Dene Michael.

Chapter 1

The early days

My story begins when I was born in St. James' Hospital, Leeds 14th December, 1956, (I had many visits here throughout my life).

My parents at this time lived and worked in Roundhay, Leeds. They had The Roundhay Park Cafe and worked very hard running the business there as well as bringing me up. My earliest memory of this time was being in my pram' outside in the sunshine of this wonderful place. People used to come up to my pram and look in at me, they usually say "what a lovely baby" don't they? But, in my case they used to look in and say "ohhh.. what a lovely pram!!!!" Ha, ha.. first gag of many to come.

I remember Mum and Dad taking me for walks to the public gardens opposite, to feed the ducks and go for lovely walks around the park. And in the winter months going sledging down Hill-60, as I approached the age of 3 years old.

After selling the business, due to the pressure of work and bringing me up, we then moved to a terrace house in Harehills, Leeds, (Luxor View). They thought they were moving into a detached house, but it was just coming away from the others in the row.. ha ha.. told you, many gags to come!

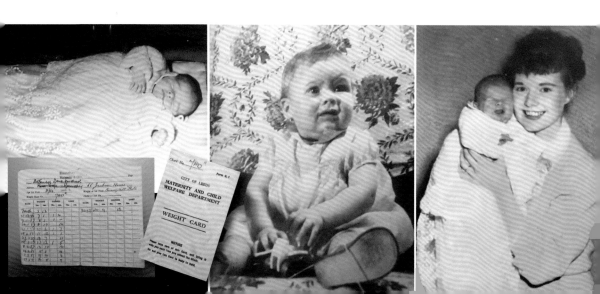

One of my memories of Luxor View was when I first used to sing in the street with my arms open to all the neighbours. I fondly remember BO BO, our next door neighbour and Mrs Woodhead, they used to say to me "come on Dene, sing for us" and I used to sing 'I know what it means' by Perry Como, one of my fathers favourite singers, who he used to impersonate.

This was the time I remember being introduced to God, as my parents were keen church goers. Mum and Dad met in church.

When Mum took me out for walks in my pushchair, I used to say "can we go see Jesus, please?" I was fascinated with his big statue outside the church. I can also remember being with Mum and Dad at church one day watching them have Holy Communion and I shouted out… "can I have a biscuit as well?".. oh well, I was only 3 at the time!

We then moved to Scholes, still in the outskirts of Leeds, to a brand new bungalow. At first I didn't like it there and asked Mum and Dad "can we go back to live in that mucky house" - lol.

After living there for quite a while I became used to it, and started my schooling at Scholes Primary School, where I met lots of friends and became popular with my school mates, because I was very musical. My first band was formed here. We played often in the school and the village hall. I remember doing my first outside concert here for school sports day, as they let us perform at this event.

I can remember building my first go-cart (bogey) there, with my Dad. I used to turn it on its side and grab the wheels and pretend to be a bus driver. (I did actually become one for a while, later in my life).

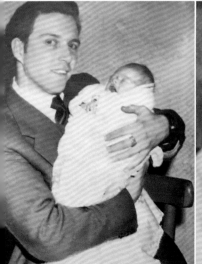

Around the age of 4 is the time when we found out I had asthma.. I was allergic to animals. I was devastated, as I loved pets.

As I have gotten older I'm pleased to say my asthma has started to go away.

Also, at this time, I had my appendix out. I think this could have triggered my asthma, as I was very distrought, as this was my very first time in hospital, left alone away from my parents.

At the age of 6 my brother Simon was born. I remember praying to God that if Mum was having a girl could he change it into a boy please, because I wanted a brother. I was so pleased it turned out to be a boy and thanked God for giving me a baby brother.

My brother Simon, I am so proud of you. Simon has done very well in his career as a professional Golfer.

We had so many happy memories growing up and travelling the world as a family, which I will be telling you about later in this book.

I remember Mum and Dad having a Bedford Dormobile, at this time. We used to go in it for family holidays to Cornwall, etc.- so many happy times.

Back to the bungalow now...

I can remember being in this bungalow on Thursday nights waiting for Dad to come home from work as it was payday for him and he always brought home sweets and treats for us as we sat down to watch Top of the Pops.

This is where I started having the dream of being a pop star, probably around the age of 7. And, of course, as you know, I did!

Happy memories of Scholes, which we return to later in the book.

Dene & brother Simon

Grandad William

Grandad William, Grandma Kate, Mum, Dad & me

Grandma Annie and Grandad Wilfred

Chapter 2

From Leeds to Leicestershire

In 1967 our family moved to Leicestershire to run a club called Ibstock British Legion Club, (no longer there, sadly, it's now a block of flats).

My mother and father became the steward and stewardess of this, then very popular, Working Men's Club. It was here, where I used to watch all the visiting cabaret acts.

I was too young to actually go into the concert room, but I used to watch them from outside the doors in the private corridor. I also used to watch the organist and drummer. That was it, I was hooked on wanting to learn to play the organ and used to sneak in the concert room when it was closed and jump on to the organ and I started to learn to play it myself by ear. Our organist at the time realised someone had been playing the organ when he wasn't there. I had to own up!!!! He asked me to play what I had learnt so far to him on the organ. He said if he gave me lessons I would be playing it to a very high standard within 6 months.

I then moved to playing the drums when the room was closed and the same thing happened there, our drummer gave me some lessons also.

The thing I remember of our time

Dad, Mum and me

Dene Clowning around

at Ibstock was changing schools. I attended Coalville Convent school (remember my parents were keen Catholics). It was here I was taught by Nuns. They taught me how to sing in harmony in the choir, and seeing a talent in me they spent quite a lot of time nurturing me into singing solo. I was 10 years old at this time.

I can also remember going on the school trip to Alton Towers, we were all singing on the coach on the way there and back, I was very close to the Mother Superior. I can remember playing football with all the Nuns.. they were great fun.

My brother Simon was 4 at the time and I was 10 and I can remember on Sunday afternoons Mum and Dad had a few hours off from the club, so we used to jump in the car and head down the motorway to the services at Leicester Forrest East for our

Sunday lunch. The car we had at the time had a speedometer that changed colour, from amber to green, then from green to Red, as the car travelled faster! I can remember shouting out in the back seat and watching the speedo.. "Dad make it go red"... ha, ha, this is where I think I got my passion for motor racing (more to come on this later in the book).

Just before we left the club to move to Australia, I can remember the club having thousands spent on 'refurbing' it, as I say (you might say 'refurbishing').

Simon and I liked to sit talking to the workmen and were very interested in how they did the job. I can remember them installing a wooden dance floor and a new lighting system and a glass mirror ball in the centre that used to revolve, I was enthralled by it all, as was my brother Simon.

DENE STARTED CHATTING GIRLS UP AT A VERY YOUNG AGE !!!

Dene and his brother Simon

Chapter 3

£10 Poms off to Australia. 1968

My family headed down to Southampton to join a ship, the Ellinis, a Greek liner on a voyage which will take us 6 weeks to arrive there into Sydney, Australia.

We as a family emigrated, as many from the UK did at the time, on a £10 passage. Yes, that's all it cost at the time, as the Australian government were looking for specialist tradesmen to build up the economy in Australia.

My father Eric had such skills, as he had worked in a specialist heat treatment department (hardening the steel) in the royal ordinance factory, years before, making fighter tanks for the Government in England. Eric returns to work here again in later years.

So, here we are, on ship saying goodbye to my grand parents William Betteridge, Katherine (Kate) Betteridge, Wilfred Croft and Anne Croft. It was very sad at the time, leaving them behind, whilst we went off to make a new life for ourselves in another country on the other side of the world. We missed them all tremendously, as there was no internet, etc. at the time; we had to rely on letters through the post to communicate, which would take weeks to arrive.

So off we went, setting sail half way around the world. I can remember the rough seas and entertaining the guests as I became involved in the

Me Mum & Simon

Dene learns to play the guitar

entertainment on ship. I was asked to do the DJ show of an evening, and then when they found out I could sing I was invited to perform some songs with the band, 'The Costa Prendes Orchestra'. This would be my first cruise ship performance, of many, with many more in years to come.

It seemed to take forever to get to Australia, I must have visited the cinema on ship 50 times to watch the film The Sound of Music with Julie Andrews etc. it had just been released earlier that year.

My brother Simon was 5 years old by this time and he had to go to school on ship, I was 11 so did not have to attend school at this time.

I can remember visiting various countries on the way to Sydney, Las Palmas in particular was the first time I had experienced heat like that. Our journey got hotter and hotter as we travelled to other countries like Cape Town in South Africa. This is where I first experienced seeing the poverty of a third world country, with beggers lined up at the side of the ship as we disembarked, whilst they re-fuelled the ship and stocked up on fresh food.

I can remember rats and mice running wild around the docks. We did get to see Table Top Mountain… what a view that was. Although the service was very slow here I can remember waiting ages to be served with a drink, ha, ha. What a great experience though to see all these wonderful places.

I can remember when we travelled across the Indian Ocean, my brother Simon was crying with the heat, it was unbearable to us as we were not used to it.

On a later voyage home we visited New York and experienced going up the Empire State building for the first time, visiting China Town, and being told to walk along the edge of the kerb as we were liable to be mugged if we walked to close to the shop doorways in the streets of

Dene, Simon & mum

Dene the on-board entertainment

New York. Also, I remember buying an Elvis record from a record shop that was very rare. I later gave it to my Roadie, Tommy Hall, as he was a massive Elvis fan.

Eventually arriving in Sydney, I can remember my uncle coming to meet us off the ship as my aunts, uncles and cousins, were already there. We stayed with them for a while, whilst my Dads job started and we eventually found our own place to live.

My uncle Brian taught me how to barbecue, which became very helpful when I lived in Spain, later in life. He also took me to Bondi Beach, where I learned to surf and had life saving lessons. Happy times!

My other interests in Australia included Rugby, where I joined a team and used to play on a weekend, and I also learnt to ice speed skate in Sydney and joined the team there as a teenager. I was quite good at this and could jump over 6 barrels on the barrel

jumping section of ice skating.

I have many fond memories of being in Australia, I was enjoying life, enjoying High School, Randwick Boys High, where my best pal was Gary Pankhurst, who played Sonny Hammond in 'Skippy the bush Kangaroo' TV programme. We sat next to each other in school and became great friends.

I had my paper round to do early mornings and after school, where my brother used to come and help me, as its very different doing a paper round in Oz, as the houses are so far apart from each other. So I used to have a wheel barrow to take them in for delivery, a whistle, and lots of elastic bands. I had to roll the papers up with the elastic band, so I could throw them over the hedges or walls and blow my whistle to tell the customer in the house it had been delivered, (couldn't do that in the UK they would be wet through, lol). We lived in Clovelly at the time near Coodgey and Bondi

Dene with a rugby mate

Dene at rugby

Dene with mum & dad

Beach, that's where my paper round ended each day. I joined the Air Cadets there in Clovelly.. again great times, absolutely loved it.

My brother Simon and I loved skateboarding and would skate everywhere we could. We saw lots of snakeskins as we skated around, as they used to shed a lot around where we played, but we were very fortunate not to get bitten. Also, I was very wary of red backed spiders, as, if you were bitten by one of these, you only had ten minutes to live if you were not next to somewhere with the vaccine to neutralise the venom. We walked around bare foot most of the time or if not, then in flip flops. I'm quite surprised we didn't get bitten by anything all the time we were there. We met lots of friends in Australia and ate lots of Lollys (sweets) and chips, (crisps), we would often go to the city and visit 'Luna Park' which was a funpark with great rides and rollercoasters etc., many happy memories here.

I was very fortunate also to visit the Snowy Mountains (Blue mountains) with my school.. again, what an experience. Just after this, I made my first ever record in Sydney. I recorded a song I'd written myself, 'There once was a boy who went sailing'... with 'Scarborough Fair' on the flip side. Also, a version of 'Hey Jude'. That was the start of my recording career at the age of 13.

I performed in shopping centres and on the beach, many times in Australia. When we left to come back to the UK, I said to all my friends "you haven't got rid of me!" I left them all one of my recent recordings each.. lol.

We had a letter from my grand parents saying my grandad was very ill and my father Eric was very worried about them, so we decided to come back to England to look after them. We said our goodbyes to our family and friends in Australia, then off we sailed again, back to Blighty.

Dene with mates near Bondi beach

Dene with his 'Aussie' mates

Chapter 4

Back to good old Blighty - 1970s

Off we go back to the ship, onboard for another 6 weeks travelling, cruising the waves. It was quite rough seas as I recall. One particular evening I remember singing on stage and the boat tipped to the side and a man came sliding across the stage area and grabbed my microphone stand to try and stop himself, then as the boat tipped the other way he brought it back to me and I carried on singing, it was as though it was part of my act, lol. The audience were laughing so much.

That same evening back at our cabin I can remember my father, Eric, leaning over the toilet being sick and his false teeth dropped out into the toilet bowl and the boat tipped again very heavily and put Dad off balance and he grabbed the toilet flush to stop himself falling and guess what? The teeth were flushed away to sea. It wasn't funny at the time, but we laugh about it now.

Once again, I was featured very heavily in the entertainment programme on board ship. I was learning my trade and was very popular with the passengers, (my first taste of fame), well, I did have a captive audience for 6 weeks, ha, ha.

When we arrived back at Southampton, England, I can remember my father as we walked

Dene at a party

Grandad Wilfred Croft

Dene family Sydney

down the gang plank onto English soil again, getting on all fours and kissing the ground, ha ha, he was so happy to be home!

My grandfather, Wilfred Croft, picked us up from the docks - we were so pleased to see him.

We travelled back up north and when we stopped at the services we were looked at very strangely as we had no shoes on! (we were so used to walking around with no shoes in Australia).

It seemed like forever our trip back up north to Leeds.

It was now 1970 and I was taking notice of the pop charts by now. My first memory of hearing music on the radio on the way back on the motorway was 'In The Summertime' by Mungo Jerry (who I would meet later on in life).

We stayed with my grandparents, Wilfred and Anne Croft, at the Manston Hotel, which they ran in Crossgates, Leeds, until we found a suitable house for us to live in.

My memories of my other grandparents (my Dad's Mum and Dad), William and Kate Betteridge, were of much love and fond memories as with my Mum's parents.

My grand father, William, had health problems, as I recall. He was suffering from TB. He had been a coal miner in early life and had coal dust on his lungs. I can remember having to have tests to see if any of us in the family had it and having vaccines, just in case we were destined to get it.

My grandad, William (Bill), used to love a bet on the horses, in fact he gave all his money to sick animals! He didn't know they were sick when he was betting on them, ha, ha.. about time for another joke..lol. I can remember him sending my grandma, Kate, to to the book makers in Seacroft every day to put his bets on. Grandma used to take ages as she liked talking to everyone on the way.. lol. He used to say "where have you

Ellinis

been Kate? Gabbing again I bet."
We had some great times with my
grand parents, I can remember
going to the east coast and sitting
on the beach with them with
overcoats on and grandad had
his flat cap on.. (seen on page 11)
happy times and memories.

I went to 'Sherburn High School'
from here, where I wasn't very

happy. The other kids (male) were
very jealous of me as I spoke with
an Australian accent.

We moved back to Scholes
Rakehill Road, Leeds. This is where
I took an apprentice job on a
Saturday morning and during
school holidays at the White Tower
Garage, on the York Road, A64.

Dene & Colin at a Black Lace PA

Dene, mum, dad, Simon at Butlins

Mum, dad, Dene & Simon cruise stc

Chapter 5

Last days of school and my first job.

I recall that our time at Rakehill Road was quite fun. This is where I finished off my school years at Sherburn High School, quite a long way from where we lived in Scholes. I had to travel by school bus, which took around an hour each way.

I was very popular with the girls at this time, as I said before, I had this Australian accent and they loved it! I was also very popular with the music department, because I had been used to performing on the cruise ships etc. and they saw big potential in me as a performer. I was even very popular in the drama department, as I could also act quite well too. By the way, do you know what my favourite musical instrument was at school? The dinner bell.. Lol.

My hobby at the time was metalwork and I made a go cart with a fully working engine, with my teachers help. I was so proud of it and it put me in good stead for my mechanics job coming soon.

I can remember being bullied here by the boys as they were so jealous of me. I had to fight the cock of the school brothers to stop them bullying me. So one lunchtime it was arranged we would have a good scrap near the tennis courts. It wasn't really fair as the two of them were fighting with me at the same

Mum & Dad

Dad at villa in Spain

time. I can remember being very annoyed and so angry I don't know where I got the strength from, but I managed to beat them very badly and gave them both a bloody nose and split one of their heads open.. I was in trouble!!!! Marched to the headmasters office, I got a good caning across my hands. I left school just after that as I had a job to go to, where I was training to be a mechanic on Saturday mornings and also I had joined a band, 'Crushed Velvet'.. my father Eric was our manager. We were doing the clubs around Yorkshire. Our agent was Norman Thewlis of Dewsbury, Yorkshire. Norman asked my Dad if he could be our agent and he arranged a showcase for us to perform in the Working Men's Clubs around Yorkshire.

Two of the band members worked with me at the garage in the paint department (Tommy Hunt - lead guitarist and Paul Meston - bass guitar). Also in the band was a great friend of mine, Tommy Whittaker. Drummer, Tommy, was a great character and fantastic drummer, he did a mean drum solo on 'Wipeout' and used to turn up to gigs on his vespa scooter, and Simon Rounding, rhythm guitarist, who lived out at Sherburn, where I went to school, were also part of the group. Simon later became a solicitor.

We used to play all over Yorkshire, at the time, in the Working Mens Clubs, Holiday Parks and Shopping Centres. I remember one day, my Dad had to lock me in the van as the screaming girls were trying to get to me, and the van was shaking side to side with them trying to get at me.. lol. It was scary. A few days later they found out where I lived in Rakehill Road and they camped out in tents in the Garden. My Mum went out to them and asked them what they were doing? They said 'we are waiting for Dene', so

Mum and dad back group

THE CRUSH VELVET GROUP: Seated, Paul Meston. Left to right Whittaker, Mrs. Anne Betteridge and Dene Betteridge. Another

Crushed Velvet

she made them all a cup of tea. I was at work in the garage at the time.

Crushed Velvet was very popular, we did a lot of the Shadows songs and tunes (lots of instrumentals), Tommy could make his guitar play just like Hank Marvins. We had the sound, it was great. We had a summer season at the east coast and Sea Farm holiday camp the entertainment manager was Harry Speight, a fantastic piano player, as I remember. Slade and Alice Cooper were very big at the time so we used to cover their songs also and whatever was in the charts. We all had day jobs at the time, so we were very tired with all the travelling back and forth to the east coast, we did it for 3 years running.

We also had fun at the garage. They took the Michael out of me, with me being only 16 at the time and learning the trade. I can remember my boss, Graham Wagstaff, and Brian Thompson sending me to the paint department in the garage to ask the boss Bob if I could have a long stand. He said of course, just wait there. I said ok, and after about 15 mins I asked again for the long stand and they all started laughing they said your having it.. lol. They also sent me for a bucket of tartan paint.. lol.

White Tower Garage had the contract to service and repair the trucks and lorries at Crown Paints on Seacroft Ring Road. I think there were around 20 of them to work on, so we were very busy with the contract keeping them all running. I was 16 and this is when I learnt to drive the Artics (articulated trucks), I had to, because there was sometimes no one else to move them in and out of the garage to service them. I can remember one day driving one back to the depot at Seacroft because the others were busy with breakdowns etc., as we had also the contract for the RAC and the AA. Mum and Dad were driving the other way in their car and Mum said to Dad "I'm sure thats our Dene driving that big truck", and Dad said "it can't be, he's only 16 and doesn't have a licence." Mum was right, it was me. I also drove the breakdown truck for the accident or breakdown for RAC and AA.

My first job was a car accident (head on collision), I had to go and clear the road of smashed cars, it was awful seeing all the blood and teeth etc., embedded into the dash board.

I didn't want to go to anymore, but went to many, before I left the garage to go pro.

In 1974 we moved to Green Court, in Scholes, as the other house was full of damp by this time. Many happy memories though from Rakehill Road.

Dene with
Neil Hardcastle
at Hastings Haven

Chapter

Going pro out on the road with the bands.

Late 1974, we moved to Green Court, Scholes, which is where I learned from Mum how to iron, cook, wash my clothes etc., in preparation for going out on the road, touring. Also, I worked for Rumbellows electrical shop, in Crossgates, Leeds. I used to deliver and install televisions, washing machines, cookers etc., etc. It was during the time I was working here when I had a very bad car accident, which I will tell you about later in the book.

My father was now working at the Royal Ordnance factory, in Crossgates, Leeds, making fighter tanks again. He introduced me to some of his workmates, Andy Doran and Billy Young, that were in a 9 piece soul band at the time, called 'Clandestine

Root' who were in need of a front man/singer. I auditioned on the Wednesday and started singing with them on the following Saturday. OMG.. did they show me some things in life! They took me out for my 17th birthday to the Beerkeller, in Leeds city centre, near the Merrion Centre. They all bought me a stein each.. I was so drunk, they had to carry me home and I was up being sick all night with my head down the toilet. Never again!!

They also introduced me to Winnie, a groupie girl from Doncaster, she used to follow us around everytime we were in the area of Doncaster! Enough said! There were many experiences of Gropies.. sorry, Groupies, at this time, as I looked like Donny Osmond. The girls were a plenty.

The Band were awesome. With a four piece brass section, we did all the soul classics and had a great show. One Christmas, the whole band dressed up in fancy dress Santa suits. I, of course, being the front man, had to dress up as the fairy on the tree.. lol. By the time we got to New Years Eve there were bits missing from the costumes as we had worn them all through the Christmas period. Arms missing, legs torn and the beards were all tatty, so we decided to wear them on the way back home from the gig in Doncaster, of course Winnie would have been there. So we stopped at the 40s services on the A1, where a lot of the bands stopped in those days, for a bite to eat on the way home. It was so funny for the customers seeing 8 Santas walking in, with me (the fairy) at the back, all in line.

After we had our food we all started ripping the suits off each other, it was so funny. I have fond memories of working with Clandestine Root, so many laughs and great fun and the experience of working with these great musicians, Andy Doran, Billy Young, Mick Reynolds, Ray Burton, Ian Bowden, Stan le Bone, Tony Swaine (Tony used to like to bring his own lunchbox to work with him, he used to eat bulls knob (ha ha, yes you read that right, it's a Yorkshire delicacy), he was the spit

of Elvis, "wanna say, I wanna say"), Pete Waterhouse (who later went to live in Texas).. oh, and me!

Just before we split our guitarist decided to leave so the lads said to me, "your mate Alan isn't working at the moment is he?" Alan was between bands, so I phoned him up and said to Alan, "how would you like to join Clandestine Root? He said, "yes, brilliant". He then said, "when do you want me to join". I said, "tomorrow, we have a gig". So he

Alan Barton

Clandestine Root

stayed up all night learning the parts. It was Alan Barton, later to be Black Lace.

We used to travel in a long wheel base, Ford Transit van, that kept breaking down. We all used to chip in 50 pence a week to keep it going.

We once or twice broke down on the motorway and Mick Reynolds was a real joker.. when the RAC came to give us a tow, off the motorway, Mick tied the tow rope to the wing mirror and the RAC man just looked at us all daft. Happy memories again.

When Clandestine Root split up, a few of us formed another band called 'Sunny' and then later 'Splitz'. Sunny members were Ian Bowden, Mick Reynolds, Bill White, Mick Holland and me.

Splitz members were Johnny Bell, Steve Leathley, Ian Bowden, Mick Holland and me.

We won a competition at Batley Variety Club with Splitz, for best band, and won a recording contract and a weeks performance at the world famous Batley Variety Club and a trip to see the Stylistics at Manchester Free Trade Hall.. they were with the same record company. We recorded a version of Dancing Cheek to Cheek.

We toured all over the country with these bands and became very popular, we were never out of work. We could work 7 nights a week if we wanted to and Sunday afternoon, lol. We were doing 10 day runs in the North East, Scotland and Wales.

Chapter 7

Tragedy strikes (The car crash)

November the 9th 1974, I was delivering a TV for Rumbelows, when tradgedy struck for the first time in my life. 5.50pm, I was on the way back from a delivery to meet the band at the van, as we always did, and I hit a lorry full on at 50mph. It was dark, the street lighting wasn't on, and it had been a very foggy and miserable day, so the lights on the lorry were not reflecting as they were full of mud and dirt and my lights were not good as they were all dirty from the bad weather. Bang!!!!!!

I was in and out of consciousness and I can remember looking down at my legs and the left one had been broken off by the knee as the engine had come through the bulk head. My left foot was on my shoulder. My fingers were all cut and broken as they had gone through the windscreen, my chin was bleeding where the steering wheel had come into me and hit my chin, and the roof had come down on my head and cracked my skull. I was in a bad way! The fire brigade had to come and cut me out of the car, it was a right off, and I nearly was as well.

I was taken to Leeds infirmary in the ambulance, blues and twos going. The paramedics did a great job keeping me alive as I was battered and had lots of broken bones. I was in intensive care for quite a while. The band

Sus

had heard the news and headed to the accident scene, as I was only 1 mile away when I hit the lorry. When they saw the state of the car they thought I wouldn't survive.

They phoned my Mum and Dad and told them the news. They came directly to the hospital to be by my side. I can also remember Johnny Bell, the drummer in Splitz, coming to see me every day, as well as my Mum and Dad - they never missed a day visiting me.

I was very lucky.. someone was watching over me. I actually had an out of body experience.. I was looking down on myself, laid on the hospital bed.

I was taken to Ward 16 and put into traction with pins and plates in my left leg. The surgeon said it would be 50-50 whether I would keep my left leg or not. They said I may not walk again unaided. Its amazing what they can do

for you when you think I may as well give up to it. I proved them wrong. It took quite a while to heal. I spent my 18th birthday in Ward 16 and also Christmas. I was allowed to come home to Green Court the following year, just before Easter. Then, I had to go to Physio every day to build up the strength in my legs again. I had to learn to walk again - it was hard work, but I got there eventually.

By the way there was an amusing moment whilst I was in the hospital the chap in the next bed to me, Fred, who was a vagrant and lived on the streets, on the day of his operation to take off his right leg when he came back from his operation I said to him as he was coming round from the anaesthetic "I have some good news and bad news for you".. I told him that they had taken the wrong leg off.. "OMG", he said, what's the good news?" I said "you see the man in the bed

ds General Infirmary

Johnny Bell

opposite, well he wants to buy your slippers!" True story, that.. he saw the funny side, eventually.

My band mates helped me a lot too, as they kept my job open for me for when I was ready to go back singing. I had to perform again and they really gave me a boost. The lads put a stool on stage for me so I could sing and perform with my plaster cast on (no dancing.. lol) but, at least I was performing again and it gave me the confidence to get better and do what I love to do.. perform on stage.

I had to regain confidence to drive again. I was so scared after my horrendous accident, but managed to build up the confidence to drive once more due to family and friends pushing me back to driving - huge thanks to them.

The thing I remember from Green Court is my brother Simon practicing his golf skills in the back garden, as it was massive, and he used to love playing football out there as well.

I also bought my first car here - a Triumph Toledo. It was my pride and joy but, unfortunately, it was stolen just a few weeks after I had bought it... I was so upset!

My friends, the Lally twins, Steven and Martin Lally and Wayne Foxhall and Paul Jaggor were my buddies at this time. We used to go everywhere together and even on holidays to Butlins Filey, (my first lads holiday). What fun we had!!!.

I was getting better after my accident and decided to go back on the road with my band. We were playing a 10 day run in the North East of England and this is where I met my first wife Susan. We met at Easington Colliery Club near Hartlepool.

Triumph Toledo

First Lad's holiday - Butlins, Filey

Easington Colliery Club

Chapter

8

My first marriage to Susan.

Susan and I started seeing each other on a regular basis. I would travel up to Hartlepool to where she was living with her parents Mary and John and brother Patrick. They were very welcoming to me and I spent a lot of my free time visiting them. Susan would come with me on my gigs, when she could, as she worked full time in a factory in Hartlepool. Susan would come on her time off to Leeds to visit me and my family and stay for the weekends. My family were very fond of her and still are to this day. We fell in love and were married in Hartlepool in the Catholic church there.

I even wore a white suit for my first wedding. 6 months before we were married I had to do a summer season in Clacton with my band Splitz at Butlins. We had some wonderful times there, I met Johnny Laff there and we became good friends and still are to this day.

It was very hard when you're away from each other for such a long time. Susan and I, we were very young though and we got through it. The night before our wedding, the band and I travelled all the way from Clacton up to Hartlepool in our band van. It was some trip, I can tell you, as we had to perform on stage the night before the wedding. After the wedding ceremony and 'do' on our wedding day, we had

First Wife Susan

Johnny Laff

Dene in make at Emmerd

to go straight back to Clacton to finish off our summer season. Times were hard then, as we were trying to get our first house together! We did this as I was given a compensation cheque after my car accident for a deposit on our new Barratt home in Garforth, Leeds.

The band decided it wasn't viable now to bo professional as we were all in relationships and didn't want to be away from home anymore, so I then went solo and did extra work at ITV and Granada Television to earn some extra cash to pay the mortgage. This is where I met my good friend, Graham Thornton, he was a runner for Emmerdale Farm and various TV shows at Yorkshire Television, I'm sure this is why I had lots of work, including 'Only when I Laugh', Emmerdale Farm' as a regular, 'Last of the Summer Wine', '321', and many more. I also was a regular in 'Coronation Street' at this time. This was early 1980's

by now, I can remember, as my brother Simon had just turned pro as a professional golfer, and Mum and Dad had moved by now to Barwick in Elmet, Leeds, to '52 The Boyle', a lovely cottage. I'm reminded of a time when I came home from work and found my mother sat with her feet in a bowl of disinfectant (it was around the time of the Foot & Mouth disease scare). I said 'mother what are you doing?' she said, 'well Emmerdale Farm's coming on the television soon, and I'm not taking any chances!!".. Lol.

We spent may happy years at this time. My first daughter Claire and my first son Christopher were born when we lived in Garforth. I met my Manager, Michael David, at this time too. He had faith in me and took me on his books and kept me in work around the Working Mens Clubs and Holiday Parks, etc. I can particularly remember Michael securing a gig for me in a theatre in Rhyll,

Michael David

Daughter Claire and son Chris

North Wales, with the hit group at the time, Hot chocolate. We arrived for a sound check and I used backing tracks at the time. My sound was amazing through the bands PA system, I was very happy, the best I had ever sounded.

I remember the producer of the show came running down from the rear of the theatre and stopped me half way through my sound check and said, "This isn't what we want!!!!! You sound too good!!! We just want someone to go on and strum a few tunes to bore the audience before Hot Chocolate come on, don't you just have a guitar with you?"

Luckily, I had one in the boot of my car, so said "yes I can do that". So it was up to me now to open the show for 20 minutes just with my guitar. The theatre was packed and I brought the house down!!! I received a standing ovation, ha, ha. Needless to say I didn't get a booking with Hot Chocolate again, as I took the limelight away from them.

Later in my career I played the same theatre as a headliner with Black Lace.. it felt good.

Iconic school disco anthem set for re-release after catchy song poll

Come on and do the Conga...again

SEASIDE CONGA: Black Lace in Blackpool. Left, Dene Michael and Alan Barton in their heyday

BY STUART ROBINSON

IT'S been a cheesy favourite with the DJs at school discos for generations and a tune party-goers will literally line up to have a dance to.

Now 90s anthem *Do the Conga* by Yorkshire legends Black Lace is set for a big re-release after being voted one of the catchiest tunes of all time.

Black Lace, who hail from Leeds and Wakefield, yesterday announced they were set to give the former top ten hit another outing following the poll, which saw the tune come in second just behind 90s hit *MMMBop* by Hanson.

First released in 1994, *Do The Conga* has enjoyed a recent mini-revival thanks to its appearance in a TV advert for train travel.

Singer Dene Michael said: *Do the Conga* is such a fun, upbeat song and we're delighted it's seeing a revival

Whatever age you are or walk of life you're from, it's a song that's bound to put a smile on your face and get you moving. It might however get stuck in your head - we make absolutely no apology for how catchy it is!"

It was joined on the list by classic party anthems *Come on Eileen* by Dexy's Midnight Runners, *The Birdie Song* by The Tweets and *Club Tropicana* by Wham. They were placed alongside

more recent favourites like 2002's *The Ketchup Song* by Las Ketchup and *Saturday Night* by Whigfield.

The results also revealed one in ten people find themselves with a song stuck in their head every day and almost a quarter can take a whole day to get rid of it.

Shamefully two thirds of those surveyed knew the full accompanying dance routine to the *Macarena*.

The top ten, from one to ten was: Hanson, *MMMBop*; Black Lace, *Do the Conga*; Dexy's Midnight Runners, *Come on Eileen*; Chesney Hawkes, *The One and Only*; The Tweets, *The Birdie Song*; Red-nex, *Cotton Eye Joe*; Las Ketchup, *The Ketchup Song*; Wham, *Club Tropicana*; Whigfield, *Saturday Night*; Bucks Fizz, *Making Your Mind Up*; 1981 *Do the Conga* is available to download from iTunes.

stuart.robinson@ypn.co.uk

Chance find brings star's music back

A LONG-LOST solo album by Black Lace star Alan Barton is finally set to see the light of day thanks to his son Dean Barton and his band Spirit of Smokie have discovered Alan's vocals on old tapes that had been left collecting dust for 13 years.

The group will celebrate the launch of its album, called Room With A View, with a gig in Kirkhamgate, Wakefield. Alan died in a bus crash in Germany while on tour with Smokie in 1995. Dean, 34, of Mirfield, said: "We thought at first it

would just go out to family and friends as a nice tribute for my dad. But we've really done him proud by getting the album to sound like it does. This is just what he would have wanted." The band will play at Kirkhamgate Village Hall on Friday, from 7pm.

FOUND: Dean Barton, Graham Kearns and Andy Whelan

Tickets, costing £12, can be bought by calling 01924 366804 or 07830 000042.

ROUND TOWN NEWS

Edition 320 Friday 25th November - Thursday 1st December 2005 www.roundtownnews.com

50,000 COPIES AND OVER 125,000 READERS EVERY WEEK!

ALFAZ EX-PAT RELEASES CHARITY RECORD

Alfaz del Pi resident and ex Black Lace pop singer, Dene Michael, was shown nationally on the BBC's 'Children In Need' last Friday singing his new double 'A' side single, 'What Colour Is The Wind?' and 'Dance With My Father'. Dene along with keyboard wizard, Dave Peterson, had been filmed performing the songs at Tony Hay/Round Town News's spectacular CIN concert at Benidorm Palace on 6th November.

Continued on page 3

Chapter

9

Becoming a dad for the first time and the struggles of parenthood

Susan and I were together for 7 years. Our children Claire and Christopher were born in 1979 and 1981 respectively. It was a very hard time, as I can remember struggling to make ends meet, as in January, February and March of each season, work was very scarce - singing until the holiday camps opened up for summer season etc.

I used to work at Walliss Holiday Camp, Cayton Bay, near Scarborough, for quite a few seasons. Its now called Haven Holidays, Cayton Bay.

Claire was just a toddler at this time and I remember taking her with us on Summer Season and we stayed in a caravan behind the clubhouse in the entertainers

accommodation. It was here I met Dave and Graham Pinkney and his band and did the Cabaret show each evening. They were very accomplished musicians, I became very friendly with Kevin Leach the keyboard player. We used to write songs together and record demos. We also formed The Blue Movies band and became very popular in the Scarborough area. I also became very friendly with the entertainers upstairs, Barbara and Ken Thompson, in the Rondezvous Lounge, and when Ken died Philip Pentney took Kens place on drums.

It was here I met and became friends with Stan Richards (Seth Armstrong) from Emmerdale. He played the piano and told some very funny jokes.

Also, whilst performing at Wallis's I was very fortunate to work with Cheekita Scales and Melody Scales her daughter. They both taught me a lot about Pantomime. I worked with them in a production show called 'Oliver' - I played Mr. Bumble. This put me in good stead for performing in Panto later in life.

My wife Susan also used to help with the entertainment in-between looking after Claire our daughter. We met some lovely friends there, including Colin and Carol Bilton from Stockton in the North East of England. I am still friends with them to this day. Christopher, my first son, was born the next year, so all the to-and-frowing had to stop. I wanted to be nearby and with my family.

So after the summer season finished we all settled back in Garforth, where I took a job as a lorry driver. I worked for Jack Fulton Frozen Value, delivering food to hospitals, old peoples homes, schools, farms, etc., etc. It was a tough time as I was still singing

solo at the weekends. I ended up hardly being with my family as it was all work, trying to earn enough money to keep us all going and pay the bills. I loved the very little time I had away from work with my family.

We had some good friends.. Alan Barton (Black Lace) and his wife Elaine were our very close friends, we spent a lot of time together with our families and children. Alan, Elaine, Susan and myself took a holiday in Paris together..I know, sounds lovely doesn't it..but no, it was a nightmare!

We drove there and we were late getting into Paris. My wife Susan was pregnant at the time and as we arrived there Susan had a miscarriage. We had to take her to hospital and struggled with the language. Susan had to stay in

Dene with Colin Bilton

hospital overnight, so we had to leave Susan there. Then when we arrived at our hotel they didn't have the correct booking for us. So Alan, Elaine and myself had to stay in one room, that's all they had with one double bed. So Elaine slept at one side of the bed Alan in the middle and me on the other side of the bed. It was so funny when we all said goodnight, Alan said "goodnight Elaine", then Elaine said "goodnight Alan", I then said "goodnight Elaine" she replied "goodnight Dene", Alan then said "goodnight Dene", I replied "goodnight Alan", it was so funny at the time, you should have seen the cleaners face as she came into the room the next morning.. lol. We had some very happy times, all of us, with the children.

We didn't have much money at the time, but we managed to take Claire and Christopher to Blackpool for a weeks holiday in a hotel on the seafront. We had a fantastic time, but had to pay the credit card bill when we arrived home, it was a real struggle to make ends meet. I was writing songs at the time and trying to get a hit record. I used to go down to London once a month or so to try and get my songs published. I trundled around various publishing companies with no luck really, but kept on trying.. it was rejection after rejection, very disheartening!

Claire was 4 years old by now and Christopher 2, I was working away all the time, back doing the 10 day runs around the country. Susan was not happy with me doing this so she used to go stay in Hartlepool with her family with the children every time I had to work away. We were drifting apart, so I decided to take a residency in Leeds, 'Tiffanys Night Club' in the Merrion Centre. I joined the resident band 'Freeway', led by Bill Jessop. We played every Wednesday, Thursday, Friday and Saturday evenings and I also sometimes used to double, doing the Working Mens Clubs and Pubs

CHEEKITA

BARBARA THOMPSON B KEN

Dave Pinkney, Melody Soales, Kevin Leach

- as a drummer, vocalist or solo. My roadie and good friend was Tommy Hall, a fantastic worker, nothing was too much for him, he was a very lovable character. Thanks Tommy for being there for me.

Even though I was working so much with the band and also solo, times were very hard and we still had a lot of debt. Susan and I had become different people, we were growing up and wanted different things in life, so we decided to split up. Susan would go and live in Hartlepool with our children and I would move into 52 The Boyle, in Leeds, with Mum and Dad.

I would go and visit Claire and Christopher most weeks when I had time off work and they would come to stay with me on school holidays, etc.

I missed them all so much. I can say that Susan always wanted me to see our children as much as I could - she encouraged it and it worked out well for us as we are still friends to this day. I adore Claire and Christopher and they have given me some wonderful grand children. Christopher gave me Courtney, Leah, Owen and Mason. Claire has given me Alfie and Archie. I love them all dearly.

Some of Dene's family - Nicky, Owen, Danni, Chris, Mason, Leah, Mum, Claire, Archie & Alfie & Albi the dog

Chapter 10

Becoming a pop star, the struggles of stardom and marriage to 2nd wife Lesley.

Back to Living at Mum's and being single again. I kept doing my solo show as a drummer/vocalist and about 2 years after splitting up from Susan I met Lesley at one of my gigs in Bradford, West Yorkshire.

We courted for about 6 months then we decided to buy a house together in Bradford.

I had found love again with Lesley and was very happy being with her. We adopted my manager's Alsatian dog, which later I found I was allergic to, it was so upsetting when we had to take her back to him, the dog adored us.

We struggled once again to make ends meet in this relationship as I had to pay maintenance to Susan for Claire and Christopher, which of course was my first priority, along with the mortgage and usual bills.

We were out shopping one day doing some Christmas shopping and went to visit my Mum and Dad in Leeds, and they said that John Wagstaff and Alan Barton had been phoning all afternoon (no mobile phones in those days.. lol), and it was urgent that I contacted them.

So 5.50 pm on the Friday I phoned them from my Mum and Dads.

2nd wife Lesley with baby Kelli

Dene & Colin promo shoot

Alan said they had a problem with Colin and could I join Black Lace and they wanted a meeting with me immediately. I shot off to the office and they then offered me a position as front man along with Alan.

I said to Alan "when do you want me to join?" He said "tomorrow, we are headlining at the Wakefield Theatre Club."
He'd got me back!!!
if you remember, earlier in the book I had asked him to join Clandestine Root, he'd said, "when do you want me to join" and I said "tomorrow!!!" lol.

We were up all night again learning the parts and putting a show together. It was a completely different world now as they had just been in the charts and were very famous. It changed our lives. It was like a load had been taken away from me. We were in the money and I was living life as a pop star as we were recording and doing various TV shows. I spent 6 months in the recording studio, along with Alan, making a new Album, 'Party Crazy'. It was TV advertised and our faces were never off the TV. We even recorded a film 'Rita, Sue and Bob Too' and they even made puppets of us for the TV show, 'Spitting Image'.

We were also chosen to do the official record for the World Cup in Mexico - 'Viva la Mexico'. It was all happening for us.

Lesley and I decided to have another child. Kelli was born and then we married on Kelli's first birthday.

My fourth child came along, my son Nicky, he was born just in the nick of time as Lesley went into labour when we were in Huddersfield and I had to drive her to Bradford to the hospital there and the weather was bad. We arrived just in the nick of time. Nicky was born as soon as we got to the hospital.

Life was good, we bought another

...ne on set of 'Rita, Sue & Bob Too'

Filming 'Rita, Sue & Bob Too'

house on Hunsworth Lane in Cleckheaton near Bradford.

One of my strong memories of this home was when we were in bed one evening, all the family were asleep and we were burgled. They broke into the bungalow and stole our car keys and a few other items and drove away in our cars. Frightening when you think that someone was in the next room while we were asleep. We decided to move away from that area as quite a few robberies were happening there. So we moved to Bolling Hall Road, still in Bradford.

We opened a shop for my wife Lesley called 'Yuppy Kidz' selling childrens clothing and designer baby items. Unfortunately, we were only open for around 9 months, as it just wasn't working in that area. i think it really needed to be in London or Leeds for it to work.

Alan Barton had left Black Lace to become lead singer with Smokie and Colin had come back into

Black Lace, at this time, and we recorded various songs together at a good friends studio, 'Academy Studio', owned by Keith Appleton. We recorded the Blue album there.

I became good friends with Keith and became a studio engineer there and learned the ins and outs of recording. I have recorded many songs at Keiths and still work with him to this day. Keith now has his own TV and Video company. I have done lots of filming with Keith, I was introduced to Jem Frazer through Keith. Lots of stories to tell about Jem later in the book.

Lesley and I bought a static holiday home in Flamingoland where I was doing some solo shows. We had many happy times there at Flamingoland and the children loved it there. It was here I wrote 'The Music Man' which became a massive hit for us. We did lots of the Radio 1 Roadshows etc., we were promoting it all over the UK and Spain.

I AM THE MUSIC MAN

THE DENE MICHAEL SHOW

I left Black Lace at this time as the pressures of touring had gotten too much for us. We were touring around the Butlins holiday camps. Mondays were our only day off!!! Tuesdays we would set off to Aire in Scotland and do a show there, then we would travel on Wednesday mornings to Pwllheli in Wales to do our show. Thursdays we would travel to Skegness, do our show there, then Fridays were Bognor Regis. Saturdays we had to travel to Minehead, do the show then Sunday up to Great Yarmouth then we would to travel back through the night, back to Yorkshire for our day off on Monday, which wasn't really a day off as we would have to catch up with management meetings etc., have all our clothes washed and then repack to start back on tour again on the Tuesday. We had 16 weeks of that, can you believe!!!

We got to about 13 weeks of doing that tour and then I collapsed with exhaustion. The pressure was too much for me as I was doing most of the driving. I took some time off to recharge my body!!

I then formed another group, 'The Dene Michael Band' - with Neil Hardcastle, Trevor Baines and Peter Moore.

We toured all over the UK and Germany, doing the Army bases in Germany for a good friend Steve Fisher.

He had an entertainment agency over in Germany and we would go over many times for him.

I particularly remember one evening it was my birthday and we were booked at a very posh do for all the Army officials where they gave away a car in a raffle and various prizes including a big screen TV etc., etc. Steve said to us, "be on your best behaviour tonight as its a very important gig", so we wound him up, I pretended to be drunk as it was my birthday. Neil said to Steve "we can't go on, Dene is really drunk, he's in

Dene Michael Band

the dressing room and can hardly speak!" He came running in to the dressing room to try and sober me up, lol.

I pretended to be drunk - he was so upset!!! So I just stood up and said to Steve, "got ya!!!!" Ha, ha, it was such a good wind up, we went on stage and stormed the place for him, it was a great gig.

We ended up getting another summer season at Coombe Haven in Hastings with the band - that lasted 6 months. This is where I met my best friend Dave Jeffrey. Lesley came to visit with our children Kelli and Nicky for a few days - our marriage was just about over by then as we had drifted apart with the pressures of being away from each other so much. I should have learned my lesson by now, but music and performing was all I knew.. and was good at! We had a few more months to do at Coombe Haven after Lesley and I had split up.

One night Dave Jeffrey and I were at the bar drowning our sorrows as he had just split up from his partner too.

We got so drunk, Dave decided to put me in the back of the bin truck and drive me back to the accommodation where we were all staying, (3 caravans behind the roller sports centre at the bottom of Battle Hill, onsite).

I bought a scooter to get up and down the hill on, but that was a disaster also, as one night after the gig I was going down the hill on the scooter (which was like a ski slope by the way), I hit the kerb at the bottom of the hill and ended up in the bushes, upside down with the scooter on top of me - that was the end of that!

Dave took the scooter to repair and sell on. He did well out of it because he advertised it as being owned by an 80's pop star! He sold it straight away and got good money for it. I then bought a classic

Dene with daughter Kelli & son Nicky

Nicky & Dene

Dene and Dave Jeffrey

Jaguar car which Dave did up for me, it was fantastic! He did a great job and re-sprayed it for me.

At the end of the season I took it back up to Yorkshire and then I moved into our holiday home in Flamingo Land. Lesley stayed in our house in Bradford with our children. I used to have them come and stay with me at Flamingoland along with Claire and Christopher. I have made 2 records for The England football team. The first one was in 1986 for the World Cup in Mexico, It was called Viva la Mexico, we had to record it in various languages, I remember having interpreters in the recording studio to show us how to say the words in different languages and piece it all together word by word.

It sounded good by the time we had finished recording it. We were sponsored by Adidas and were given track suits, football shirts, trainers, hats etc. The second World Cup record, I will talk about later in the book.

Chapter 11

Flamingoland and meeting my 3rd wife Alison.

So, here I am in Flamingoland. After leaving Hastings, I had a few weeks off then was asked to become Entertainments Manager at Flamingoland, which was a big task. There were 5 venues to supply entertainment for in the evenings and I also had to run an entertainments team, including shows on the park throughout the day.

I had the help of my agent, Michael Hainsworth, to supply some great artists as visiting cabaret, so that took some pressure off me and I could concentrate on running the park entertainment and the team of dancers, singers, magicians, childrens entertainers, circus performers, etc. Also, with being in management I had to sort any problems the park had and oversee the running of everything, including the rides, rollercoasters, etc.

Trevor Pullin was my boss there, along with Mr. Gibb - they were very good to me and gave me a free hand in running all the entertainments for many years. I can remember going to other theme parks with Trevor to look at buying new rides for our park. We became very good friends.. sadly, Trevor has passed away now. Mr. Gibb was killed in a car accident.

I had many happy years with them all at Flamingoland, including meeting many friends there, including Karl Reevely, who was

Dene with Mike Hainsworth

Flamingolan

a manager. He used to help me with the entertainment and became one of the park costume characters 'Charlie Chimp'. We had lots of fun, but it was very hard work doing 14 hour days.

All 4 of my children adored being with me at Flamingoland, they had the run of the park and enjoyed going on all the rides and seeing all the shows I had put on. Claire, my eldest daughter, became part of the team as she sang on a few of my shows and also found work on the park in the daytime.

One of the ride operators, Claire Dowson, was a fantastic Jazz singer. She did a few shows for us and was very popular with our customers. So, we put a duo together and became 'Ferrari'. We ended up doing some clubs for Mike Hainsworth in the winter as well as doing Flamingoland in the summer.

Also, in the winter, we did some shows in Benidorm in Spain. Claire and I became partners and lived together for a while.

Whilst we were in Benidorm we met some great friends, Peter and Lynne Allen, they visited Benidorm quite often and still do to this day. They never missed a show if we were there at the same time. Big fans and now personal friends. Claire Dowson is also a good friend and we still keep in touch.

Around this time I was sponsored by a York garage 'D C Cooks'. They gave me a shiny red sports car to use, with my name all over it.. I felt so privileged to be driving around in my Toyota MR2.

One of my neighbours at Flamingoland were the Bennett family from Middlesborough, who came to visit a caravan they owned every week. They used to come to the clubhouse to watch my shows and Malcolm Bennett used to work on the park.

Alison Bennett used to look after her younger sister Karen and her

Dene's shiny red Toyota MR2

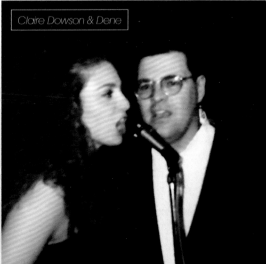

Claire Dowson & Dene

younger brother Alan and brought them to many of my shows and became very good friends with all the family. My children would play with Karen and Alan as they were much younger than Alison and Malcolm. We were all very close.

Alison was a lot younger than me, but we had a lot in common, and fell for each other. We then became a couple and Alison moved in with me in my static home on the park.

Just as we started to see each other, I had a phone call from Alan's wife Elaine, with the tragic news of the coach crash in Germany of Alan Barton and Smokie and just a few days later the death of Alan. I was distraught, as Alan was like a brother to me.. I was so upset!

I spoke with Alison and said I'm not happy here anymore, about all the travelling in the winter time, and thinking about how could I not be on the motorway every day, in so much danger of being in a car crash again, myself.

I had a call from Benidorm from one of the club owners, Brendan and Jackie Holden, I had met previously. They offered me a job in the 'Wheel Tappers and Shunters Club' with Terry King, a very funny man. I said to Alison, "how do you fancy moving out to Benidorm with me?" We hadn't been together that long and I was hoping she would say yes. Alison had been out to Spain with me a few times for my weekly visits with gigs I'd done solo, as a stand in for my good friend Jason Kane, another fine comedian, so he could go on holiday (you have to do 7 nights in Benidorm.. or did do at the time). No days off.. unless you can get someone to cover for you.

So our opportunity was there, if we wanted it..

So, we packed a few things up, loaded them into my car and off we went to Benidorm.

Dad with Peter & Lynne Allen and Alison

Chapter 12

Moving to Spain. The Kidnap. 2nd setback - boating accident.

So, we packed the car with my English TV and video, two suitcases, £500 in my wallet to get us to Benidorm to start a new life together. It was a very long trip, it took us 24 hours driving. We took the ferry from Dover to Calais, then drove and drove and drove. We stopped overnight in France, just before the border of Spain, after having driven for around 12 hours from England. Next morning, we were up early to drive another 12 hours to Benidorm. I can remember being very tired and hungry. We made it to Albir, and found a nice Chinese restaurant open, so we stopped the car and had a wonderful meal.

We then met my employers at the 'Wheel Tappers..', Brendan and Jackie, who took us to their house, where we stayed for a few days until we had all our paper work sorted out and had found an apartment to live in. We found a lovely apartment in La Cala just outside of Benidorm.. 'Living the Dream'.

We stayed there in La Cala for about 3 months, then moved closer into Benidorm, as we found the travelling in and out of Benidorm quite stressful although it was only 5 miles away. We found

Dene in his office at the Villa in Spain

Dene & Ian Rob...

a lovely apartment right on the sea front on Lavante Beach, it was wonderful. It felt like we were in heaven.. as we were 28 floors up, lol. Although, it was a nightmare if the lifts broke down, imagine having to walk up 28 flights of stairs! I remember my daughter Kelli getting stuck in the lift one day, it was frightening, for all of us.

I also remember the children using the lift to go onto the very top of Torre Levante on the roof garden, and one day I caught them smoking up there, ha, ha. It was a little hideaway for them.

My children used to love visiting us when we lived here as we were next to the beach and we had a lovely pool also, and we didn't need to drive to work as we could just take a leisurely stroll along the promenade to work. We lived here for about 4 years.

I can remember filming the video for 'Penny Arcade', one of my solo records, when we lived here

at Torre Lavante.. happy times, wonderful memories.

I met quite a lot of artists that came over from England. I was introduced to Ian Robinson by Gordon Humphries, a singer from Liverpool. He was playing in 'Shooters Bar', where we used to go and see Gordon sing and we became good friends. Ian came over for a holiday and ended up coming to live in Benidorm, the same as me.

Ian then worked at the 'Wookie Hollow', a liverpool bar, which is sadly now no longer! It's a tabac shop nowadays. We had some great shows in there, along with John Wardell, Freddy Joyce and Emma, who Ian used to duet with, calling themselves 'Flipside'.

Ian asked me to do Freddys night off, which was a Thursday evening and it just so happened to be my night off also, so hey, guess what? Yes, I ended up working my night off with Ian in the Wookie. It

n, Mum and Dene at Wookie Hollow

Dene, Alison & Dad at the boat that sank

was great fun, we used to have guest singers get up with us and we would back them doing the harmonies. All the acts used to love getting up with us.

We had lots of stars come to visit in Benidorm and we would invite them to the Wookie where they would be looked after by Carol and Brian, with free drinks and a great night out. We had the 'Drifters' on stage with us, 'Smokie', the 'Real Thing', 'The Overlanders' - in fact we had to stand Ricky Wilde on a beer crate because he was so small, so he was the same hight as the rest of us, lol.. it was a standing joke! By the way, did you know there's so many Drifters now, you can't get under the boardwalk.. lol.

Lots of the resident entertainers used to pop in to sing with us, also. Howard Burnette, was a favourite, he was known as the complete entertainer and he was also a good friend. He used to do a magic and illusion act where he

would set fire to people and paint them red. He'd also do his 'Electric Chair' act, which was very funny, and also he was a great singer.. R.I.P Howard, sadly no longer with us, along with Freddy Joyce.

Sadly lots of the acts from Benidorm from those days are no longer with us. One of our good friends, Stuart Jason, a comedian from Scotland, who had lots of friends in Benidorm at the time, passed away and we all went to his funeral. This is so funny, but true, and Stuwie would have loved it. Stuart was on his own in Benidorm and only had one sister alive who lived in Scotland, so when he passed away it was his wish to contact his sister and she would have all details of his funeral !!! So she came over to sort things out for his funeral and it was Stuart's wish to be cremated in his stage suit. Now we all worked at a place called 'Carriages' along with Lance Edwards (comedian), Cheroot (singer, comedian), Paul

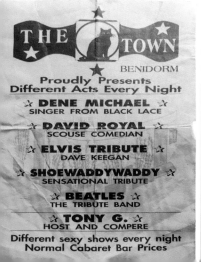

Mum, Dene, Dad - Benidorm Palc

Summers (singer), Stevie Nelson (host and compere) and me. We shared the same dressing room, so we sorted out for Stuart's sister to collect Stuart's stage suit, to take to the funeral directors.

So, we're all at the crematorium lined up to say our farewell to Stuart and in Spain they leave the lid off the coffin to say their farewells. So, Lance Edwards is in front of me in the line and sees Stuart in his coffin and says, "he's in my fucking suit", his sister had only picked up the wrong suit from the dressing room as Lance was the same build and size as Stewie. He would of seen the funny side of it though, 'cos Lance said it wouldn't be the first time someone has died in that suit.. lol.

Thats not the end of it!!! We're all sat there after the service waiting for Stu's body to go through the curtains.. and what music starts to play? AGADOO!!! Ha, ha, it was Stu's favourite song and unbeknown to anyone, he wanted to go out to Agadoo. Happy memories again.

One night, Ian said to me in the 'Wookie', "we've been asked to do a Showaddywaddy tribute with a friend called Peter King at the Benidorm Palace, for charity". So, we bought some fancy dress rock-n-roll teddy boy suits and rehearsed on a Thursday evening, and over the weeks it was coming together. We only had to do 5 songs at the charity event so we got the 5 songs really tight and sounding good. Off we go to do the gig at the 'Palace'.. we stormed it, they loved us.

We didn't know, but one of the club managers, Paco, was in the 'Palace' that night, watching us. I already worked at the 'Town', which Paco was the boss of, and he said to us "I'd love that show in the 'Town'". We said, "Paco, we only know 5 songs".. lol. He said "you better learn some more then".. and that was the birth of 'Shoewaddywaddy'. Also, the

he Town' - Dene, Paco (middle) & Bruce

Shoe Waddy Waddy tribute band

start of the very first tribute band in Benidorm. Then came a 'Take That' tribute which I put together. Ian also started a 'Bay City Rollers' tribute, then everyone jumped on the bandwagon. There were so many tributes popping up everywhere in Benidorm and we started it all off.. so blame us, lol.

I bought a boat and used to take the children out on it when they came for the 6 weeks holidays. The next disaster happened one day when we were out at sea, as the propeller picked up some debris from the sea and burnt out the engine and set it on fire somehow, and the boat started to sink, with me and my children in it.

We were all franticly trying to scoop the sea water out of the the boat.. we were sinking!!! I fired a flare into the air and luckily a Spanish fishing boat was passing nearby and came over to help us and saved our lives. We'd had lots of fun on that boat until this happened. Needless to say, the

boat was scrapped.

We then moved to a villa in 'Alfaz del Pi', again just outside of Benidorm. We had a private pool and lots of land with Orange, Lemon and Banana trees - again the children loved it there, and spent many hours in the pool and playing in the gardens picking the fruits from the trees. We also had bicycles for them to ride around our property

We had lots of friends by now and I used to invite them all to the barbecues, I used to love doing. We would set up a PA sound system outside and we'd play music and tell jokes.. very happy times.

My children loved these get to togethers, they didn't want to go home. Kelli used to cling onto me and cry, she even kept a crumb from a sandwich I had at the airport to take home with her.. bless her.

Sometimes they would come by

Dene & Bruce in Spa

car with my friend Brian Lingard from Rotherham, he used to bring English goods over for the bars in Benidorm and would squeeze the children in his car. What a trip that was for them, but worth it when they arrived.

I bought a car from England, it was quite a nice Mercedes sports car. I had it shipped over and it was delivered to me outside 'Carriages', where I worked at the time. That car was my worst nightmare!!! Unbeknown to me the car was involved with a crime gang and the gang wanted it back. They tried to steal it from me while I was away in America getting married to Alison in Las Vegas. It was in my garage locked away. It had a very complicated alarm on it. They came with a Grua (tow truck) to try and steal it from me, but with no luck.

One day I could feel these 3 men following me everywhere I was singing, and thought it was strange. They even followed me

home to see where I lived and obviously to see where the car was, as I didn't always take it into town as I sometimes used my now wife Alison's car to go down into Benidorm.

One particular night Alison came with me to my show at 'Carriages'. We decided to go down in her car and I said to Alison "your cars open", and noticed the glove compartment was hanging down. As I leant in to put my stage shirt in the back, a guy jumped up from behind the seat with full combat gear on, balaclava, the lot!! He pulled me into the car and shot a gun in the air, then held the gun to my head.

Another car came speeding up to us and two other guys jumped out of that car and pushed Alison to the ground, bundled me into that car and sped away with me in it. I had another gun held to my head and they had a big machete, threatening to cut my fingers off. It was like something out of a movie.

Dene's Villa in Spain

mum, dad & family airport pickup in Dene's Rolls Royce

They took me up the mountain and threatened they were going to put me in the boot and set fire to me if I didn't give them the keys to my car. I said I would give them to them, obviously, and arranged to leave them at an arranged place the next day.

They said I was in the wrong place at the wrong time it wasn't personal to me, but unfortunately I had bought a car that they wanted. They drove me back down the mountain, gave me the equiverlant to £10 and said now get a taxi to your work and said.. 'by the way your a good singer'!

I was asked By my good friend Mike Ellis if I could record a version of Dance with my father for his charity National Society for Children and family contact.

It was to raise money for a website to help fathers see their children after a marriage break up.I agreed and it was a big success.I was also approached by Mike to record a version of What colour is the wind? Written by a mutual friend, Charlie Landsborough again, this was a big success - so many thanks to all that bought those singles for a good cause. Dave Peterson was a big help in recording these two songs as Dave produced and played on these records and recorded them in his studio in Spain. Thank you Dave for all your hard work and friendship throughout the years.

Mike Ellis became very close to my family and we are still friends to this day.

Mike Ellis, mum, Dave Peterson, Dene & Dad

2021

COMPETITION
DRIVER | ENTRANT

Dene Michael Betteridge

RS CLUBMAN (UK ONLY)

VALID FOR CLUBMAN STATUS:
AUTOCROSS / CLUBCROSS / MINICROSS
AUTOTEST / AUTOSOLO
TRIALS, CROSS COUNTRY
ROAD & NAVIGATIONAL RALLYING
(INC. 12 CAR & SCATTER)

Licence No: 024539
Date of Birth: 14/12/1956
Expires: 31/12/2021
Starts: 01/01/2021

motor sport UK   MEMBER OF   FiA

LORD DENE MICHAEL AGADOO BETTERIDGE

This certificate entitles the assignee(s), as stipulated above, to ENGLISH STANDARD TITLE rights. The title rights assigned shall be LORD DENE MICHAEL AGADOO BETTERIDGE OF WANSLEY MANOR. In addition, LORD DENE MICHAEL AGADOO BETTERIDGE shall be assigned dedicated land within the ENGLISH ESTATE (reference number 38/9925 - members reference 101047). The associated terms and conditions document constitutes the complete legal, valid and binding terms and conditions. The assignor is Essaxen Limited and duly registered and validly existing under the laws of England. The validity, interpretation and implementation of the assignment shall be governed by the laws of the United Kingdom of Great Britain and Northern Ireland.

Chapter 13

Married Alison in Las Vegas - living the dream. Then disaster strikes again, crash landing in a plane.

Alison and I were married in Las Vegas, as I previously mentioned, in the last chapter. It was our first trip to Vegas, of many.. we ended up living there for a while. This was due to our friends we had met in 'Carriages' - John and Rose Squibb. John bred pigeons and raced them, along with his son Gary Squibb. He lived in London where he knew quite a lot of the infamous Kray family, and he was quite a character. John booked me to do a show for one of the pigeon conventions in Blackpool, which he was involved with. He introduced me to some other pigeon breeders from all over the world at this convention in Blackpool, they all loved my show. I was asked by Tom Fabey, from New Jersey, in America, to do the convention in Los Angeles, which I did. I was allowed to take Alison with me on an all paid 'working' holiday for a week.. we felt so special. It's funny how things work out, as when we were in LA, we met another pigeon breeder, Hector van Cherie, from Las Vegas. Hector was the top man

Dene & Johnny Squibb

Johnny & Rose Squibb and Dene's family

at the 'Monte Carlo' casino on the 'Strip', along with another casino in Lake Mead, next to the Hoover Dam, just outside of Las Vegas, called 'The Hacienda'. John Sqibb sorted out with Hector for me to go and work at these two casinos. I did 3 months season at the Hacienda first, then had a few weeks off before I opened at the Monte Carlo for another 3 months on the Las Vegas strip. What an experience that was!!

I met lots of the big stars appearing over there. We all used to meet at a club called the Rondezvous where we would jam and sing together after our gigs.

Lots of celebs would be in the Monte Carlo - when I was singing in the lounge bar one evening, James Brown, the soul singer, walked passed me as I was singing 'Soul Man', and he and his whole entourage stopped and listened for a while.. he smiled at me and put his thumb up, then waved and carried on walking to where he was

going - I felt sooo.. good. lol

On another evening, the movie star, Al Pacino, was sat watching me sing, along with a friend of his. I was just finishing singing 'Unchained Melody' as they sat down and was finishing my set. In my break an envelope appeared from one of the waiters, with a request written on it from Al Pacino.. it said 'please sing Unchained Melody again for my friend', which I did. Then after finishing my 2nd set another envelope was handed to me from the waiter from Al! I opened it and inside was $400 tip for me for singing Unchained Melody again.

I loved working in Vegas, one evening my friend from England, Jane McDonald, came to Vegas to do a one off TV special. It was my night off at the time so Alison and I went to see her show. We saw her coming in to do her sound check etc. in the afternoon and Jane spotted me. She came running over and said "Dene, what

Johnny Squibb with Reggie & Ronnie Kray

ny Squibb & Reggie Kray

are you doing here?" I explained how I was here for 6 months doing shows. She was made up for me, and gave us VIP tickets for the evening. We had a great time and Jane was fab, as always!

The night Alison and I were married, we were given tickets to go to the 'Motown Cafe' where the group, 'Boys 2 Men' were playing. We had front row seats, and they read out for us that we were just married and that I was a singer from England. They had had a hit with 'The end of the road', which I knew and they invited me to sing with them on stage, so I sang it with them and we brought the house down. We had free drinks all night, what a fantastic experience that was, and a night we would never forget.

We would visit Las Vegas many times after my season had finished as we had made many friends over the years and it became one of our favourite places.

One particular year we visited

Vegas we were involved in an airplane incident. We were flying from Minneapolis to Detroit on an internal flight.. disaster number 3 was just about to happen.

We took off from Minneapolis and about 20 minutes into the flight at around 2000 feet there was an explosion and we looked to the left hand side of the plane and outside the engine was on fire.

The plane was all over the place, everyone was screaming, even the air hostess was screaming and crying, saying "I don't want to die, my babys are at home".

Alison and I held hands and told each other we loved each other - we thought anytime now the plane will explode, but, unbeknown to us, these modern airplanes have extinguishers that can put out the fire, but, it didn't work straight away! So, the pilot had to dump the fuel and then try and return to the airport we had taken off from 20 minutes before. It seemed to take forever as the plane was all

Dene & Alison's wedding reception - London

Alison, Dad & Mum

over the place and was flying with one engine out of action. The pilot came on the intercom and said we would be having a very unsafe landing so to brace when he said.

Obviously, he managed to get us safely down, where the fire engines and ambulances were there to put out the fire and see to any casualties. We were all safely off the plane, down the slides, etc., and were taken into a holding area where the captain and crew were waiting to calm us all down.

We spoke to the captain and he was very apologetic and told us this had only happened once before in his flying career and he'd been flying for 40 years and was about to retire. Just our luck, we would be on this flight!!

The plane was full and they brought another plane for us to get on to continue our trip. No one wanted to get on a plane again! It was only a handful of people that would carry on to the next plane. We had to.. we had to be back in Spain for my gigs and there was no other option.

I'm still very scared of flying to this day as it never leaves your memory, what had happened to us. We were all so very lucky to survive.

Dene & 3rd wife Alison's wedding day in Las Vegas,

Chapter 14

Back to Spain. Break up with Alison.

Here we are back in Spain. After working in Vegas for 6 months, we came back to live and work again in Spain.

The season had gone quiet in Benidorm, so I was just doing the odd gig here and there. I was offered to go to Loret de Mar to star in a show at the equivalent to the 'Benidorm Palace'. So I took a few acts from Benidorm, including Howard Burnett, Ronnie Oliver, myself and Gordon James. We put on a great entertainment production of Comedy, Magic and Singing.. it was a great show in a lovely venue. We also took the show to various venues in Salou, working for George Caravannas. It was here I met Rodney Piper of RJP Entertainments.

Rodney booked me at weekends in Salou, then I would travel back to Benidorm through the night, which was a six hour drive. I still work for Rodney to this day at his re-union weekends in 'Chaplins' and 'The House of illusion'. I'm very proud to be in the RJP Hall of Fame.

Through the week, I would sell ink cartridges and do ink refills for printers. It was a business I started up with Peter King, one of the singers from Shoewaddywaddy. We also bought some donut machines that we would put onto

Dene with Rodney Piper

Burnett on stage

El Cisne Market near Benidorm, called 'Denes Dinky Donuts'.. lol. We were the first people to do the ink refill and replacement cartridges in Spain, then it seemed everyone jumped onto the band waggon again and they were everywhere. So we concentrated on the donuts, but had problems placing them at venues due to health and safety.

Also the boss of El Cisne wasn't very happy. He had a restaurant on the market selling meals and snacks, etc., when we started selling the donuts on the market we had queues of people waiting for our donuts. We were doing really well until he came and complained to us as everyone was full after eating our donuts and he wasn't selling any food.. lol. That was the end of that.

Alison and I were slowly drifting apart by now because Alison wanted to have a baby and I had had a vasectomy in previous years, after Nicky my youngest son was born. I had decided I didn't want any more children at that time.

I regretted it though, as I went for a vasectomy reversal, which didn't work because of the number of years since I had had my vasectomy. We tried IVF. That didn't work either, so we gave up after the 3rd attempt.. and about £12,000 out of pocket. We had bought an apartment to rent out in Albir, just outside of Benidorm, around this time. We lost a fortune on that also, because it was prone to flooding, unbeknown to us when we bought it.

Everything seemed to be going wrong for us. We rented the apartment out and the people that rented it ran up an electricity bill and didn't pay rent, so we gave that up as a bad idea, and just kept it for friends and family. My Mum and Dad came and stayed there, and was in two

Dene's Apartment at Albir

minds whether to rent it from us, but eventually decided otherwise as every time it rained it flooded. We lived in a villa up in the mountains in Alfaz del Pi.

I eventually started doing gigs again in Benidorm.. solo, and with 'The Elderly Brothers', a comedy duo with Ian Robinson, the Take That tribute and Showaddywaddy tribute in 'The Town' night club, where I had previously worked.

Dave Peterson, my good friend, and musical director at the time, was working in a bar called 'The Malibu'. He booked me for Sunday evenings, where he would back me live on keyboards. It was owned by a lovely Spanish family.. mother, father and their two daughters. It was a very popular place, but sadly no longer, as they sold it and it is now an Indian restaurant.

I was performing 7 nights per week doing 5 shows a night, which took its toll on my relationship with Alison and she decided she wanted to move back to England - back to Middlesborough, to her family. I remember driving her to the Airport and she said to me "I hope I'm doing the right thing, moving back to the UK, I might be making the biggest mistake in my life". I was very sad to see her go. That was in 2007. I decided to keep on doing my shows in Spain and put the apartment up for sale and I lived in the villa in Alfaz del Pi.

I went through a very bad patch of depression and anxiety at this time. Luckily, I had lots of friends that would look after me and make sure I was ok. In particular I remember Ian Robinson would come to my villa every day to make sure I was eating and he would take me out with him to different restaurants for food and invite me to go in the daytime to be with his family.. what a star.

Supermen Dene & Ian

Dave Peterson

The ELDERLY BROTHERS Live DVD Concert

THE TOWN THE ELDERLY BROTHERS VOCAL COMEDY DUO

Filmed Live at THE TOWN Benidorm

I was in Spain on my own for 2 years and made friends with a few ladies, and was introduced to my next wife Karen. I worked with her son on the circuit in Benidorm clubs and she used to come to visit him and would come to watch my shows in various clubs and she would sit with my Mum and Dad in 'The Town' when I was doing my Showaddy show.. she was very friendly with them.

When I came off stage to sit with Mum and Dad, Karen would be there getting drunk and enjoying herself. Karen's son was very jealous and didn't like the friendship developing. Karen would visit every 6 weeks or so.

I was at my villa one day and had calls from England from various TV programmes and newspapers saying they wanted Black Lace to do the Richard and Judy show, Market Kitchen, and a video to commemorate the release of 'Agadoo'.

I didn't have a singing partner at this time as Alan had died in the coach crash and Colin was living in Tenerife, so I asked Ian Robinson if he would like to do the TVs with me and record the video in Spain, which we did.

My good friend Bruce Jones (Les Battersby from 'Corrie' Coronation Street), came over to stay with me in my villa, as he was staying with me for 6 weeks or so to work with me in 'The Town' nightclub, as I was getting quite a lot of the stars to come over to appear.. including comedians such as George Roper, Ted Rodgers, Frank Carson, etc., and we used to bring stars to the Casino at Villajoyosa just outside of Benidorm. The Drifters came, Smokie, The Real Thing, and many more. I used to put on the shows once a month and they were very successful.

Bruce offered to direct the video for us and appear in it also, It was called the 'Agadoo Mambo' we

Agadoo Mambo Video shoot

Dene and Bruce at The Town, Benidorm

filmed it near my apartment in Albir, on the seafront.

Ian and I found ourselves flying back and forth to Spain, with all these appearances, and then gigs and also TV adverts, all coming from the anniversary of 'Agadoo'. So we decided to sell up and come back to good old Blighty once again.

I was asked by a very good friend of mine DJ Neil Phillips from London, to record a new World Cup song called 'We are the England fans' to the tune of my song 'I am the Music Man'. Neil came up to Castleford to record with us. We made the record at The Chairworks with Simon Humphrey producing.

It came out great and then we went to London to make the video for it on an open top bus around the city, along with quite a few guest appearances by footballers, celebrities and showbiz lookalikes.

2009, sees me starring in panto as Davinia Trollop in Cinderella at Cleethorpes, Lincolnshire. I played alongside Duncan Eyre as one of the Dames,

I had worked in Benidorm with Duncan when we were on the same bill at The Morgan Tavern, he was part of Dame Lucy bun and reg, a fantastic comedy duo. Duncan played Reg and was a very good actor, comedian.

It was very hard work doing panto as you could imagine, learning all the lines and having to do matinee performances. It was a good experience and I learned a lot from Duncan, Cheers Sis. x

I have been offered quite a few pantos since, but not been able to do them because of commitments to Black Lace, but who knows, I may do another one or two In the future.

At this time we did the Trainline Advert. We took over a whole platform in Euston Station for the whole day... 'choo choo choo come on and join the Trainline..'

Dene, Neil Phillips & Ian

Dene, Gary Lineker & Ian

Cinderella
THE UGLIE'S ARE BACK IN TOWN!

Buy Black Lace's Hit single "The Music Man" in aide of Children in Need From all good download stores From the 7th December

Dene Michael from Black Lace is **DAVINIA**

Also starring Duncan Eyre from Dame Lucy Bun & Reg as Betty

WE ARE THE ENGLAND FANS

IN SUPPORT OF
HELP *for* **HEROES**

BLACK LACE
feat. (DJ NEIL PHILIPS)

Ian, DJ Neil Philips & Dene

Dene and Ian with lookalike stunt doubles on Walkers Crisp TV Ad shoot

SAVE 43%
ON AVERAGE

Black Lace play on Trainline TV Ad

Chapter 15

Back to good old Blighty again. Black Lace comeback. The Voice UK and Marriage no.4 - the 'Agadoo' wedding.

In 2009 I rented a brand new house my agent, Mike Hainsworth, had just had built next door to him and his office at Flair Entertainments.

I was performing shows with Black Lace now in the UK and going back to Spain when I had time off from doing gigs in England. I would go across for fiestas in March and November mainly and then do the reunion weekends in Salou for Rodney Piper at 'Chaplins' and the 'House of Illusion'.

I was also offered to start working for Roland Naylor at the 'White Star' in the Marina Hotel complex in Benidorm to cover the holiday acts that were there working regular spots. It was great there, as I used to stay in the hotel, so no driving.

I took quite a lot of acts over with me to perform there, including Bruce Jones, Jenni Jaye and Chris Morris.

We were offered a TV advert for Easyjet, as they were doing a new route to Agadir in Morocco, so

Dene & Karen wedding card

Thank You

Dene
Jeni Ja

you can imagine why they asked us to do it!! Yes, we changed the lyrics to suit and off we go to Gatwick airport to record the film with the EasyJet team. Later we would record the Walkers Crisps advert with Gary Lineker with the comeback of 'Agadoo'.

After this happened, 'Ant and Dec' asked us to perform at their joint televised birthday party along with Belinda Carlisle, Ronan Keating, Pat Sharp, and Marvin Humes - wow.. what a night that was! Everyone in the audience was famous, you knew them all, although I didn't know them personally I felt as if I knew them, if you know what I mean? We got to meet a lot of the celeb's after the show and became friends with lots of them.

One day Karen turned up at my house with a suitcase and a few things. She had driven over from Stockport in Manchester, saying she had left her husband. She was in quite a state and was very upset. I took her in as a friend to start with then later we became partners and were together about a year, when a TV production company contacted us to see if we were getting married would we go on one of the shows they were putting on.. so here was the Agadoo wedding.

So when we were married in Leeds town hall a camera crew turned up along with various news teams. We were all dressed in Hawaiian shirts and attire and all the guests were too, and quite a few of the celeb's were there as well.

Bruce Jones was so funny - when it got to the part of the ceremony asking if there's anyone here who knows of any reason why these two cannot be joined in matrimony please say so now, Bruce jumped out of his seat and coughed very loudly! Everyone was laughing and then afterwards he started a conga line outside the Leeds town hall and we all did the conga back to the wedding car that

...ne, Carole Decker & Chris Morris

Dene & Belinda Carlisle

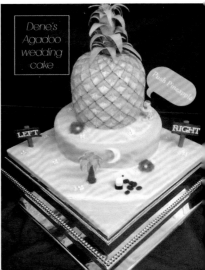
Dene's Agadoo wedding cake

was provided by our good friends Halifax Wedding Cars.

Later at the reception, in my Mum and Dads village, Barwick in Elmet near Leeds, we all partied the night away with the film crew recording everything and the village was full of paparazzi. Bruce wasn't happy, as they followed our every move!!! We even did the conga around the Maypole in the village. It was a great day though, for everyone, we even had an Agadoo wedding cake!!!

Not long after this I did some recordings for a solo album with Chris Morris from Paper Lace, which was a task in itself, as Chris lived in Bodmin, Cornwall, where his studio was, and that was a 7 hour drive from home!

It took about 6 months to record in between doing gigs, etc. It was worth it though, as the producers of 'The Voice UK' had heard one of the tracks from the solo album and contacted me and asked if I

would like to be on the show. I, of course, said yes, and performed a George Benson song 'Never give up on a good thing', which I had performed many times earlier in my career. I had a team of guests along with me to support me.

I had a very bad cold the day of recording the show and of course it was live and my voice had gone that day. They were giving me Manuka honey and lots ot water, etc., to try and get my voice working. Anyway, I managed to get through the performance, but wasn't very good. I sang in front of Tom Jones, Rita Ora, Ricky Wilson and Will.I.Am. They were all very surprised when they eventually turned around on their chairs to see me on stage in front of them. Ricky said that his band warm up with Agadoo before they do a show. Rita Ora jumped out of her seat and started to do the Agadoo dance and everyone joined in. Tom just sat there and said "the only Black Lace that

STONEY BROKE

Dene with Chris Morris

Dene with Will-I-Am on The Voice

Dene with Jem Frazer & Mum

I know is the one that Rita was wearing". And Will.I.Am didn't have a clue to who I was.. lol.

It was fun though and they invited me back to do the final and to sing Agadoo.

I was becoming very popular again with TV production companies asking me to do daytime TV and some night time peak viewing shows also.

I went to America with Karen, my daughter Claire and my grandson Alfie to do a show called 'Twin Towns' for Sky Atlantic TV. It was a reality show where family would swap houses, friends, jobs and families for a week. We were fortunate to go to Louisville in Kentucky as it was twinned with Leeds. They took us around to see the culture there and I showed the Americans how to do the Agadoo dance, they even gave me the keys to the city of Louisville on the programme and they said to me even Elton John didn't get

these when he visited, so I was honoured.

Another TV programme I did was 'May the Best House Win'. I asked my good friend, Jem Frazer, to do his 'Bubbles' character for this show. We had some laughs making it, as he was my hospitality, he dressed up as Bubbles and came with my food for my guests and served up a dead rat and jelly babies. You should have seen their faces when he turned up.

I also did a show in Benidorm called 'Living in the sun', where they came over and filmed some of the Brits. I sang my song, 'I am the music man' on there.

Karen and I did the show, 'Judge Rinder' - that was also a lot of fun. She took me on there, as I had sold our caravan and swapped it for a car. She wasn't happy.. lol.

I have been very lucky to perform on many Summer seasons in Blackpool including The Winter Gardens, Blackpool Tower, North

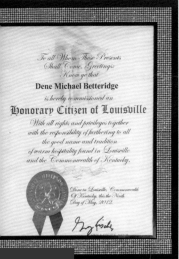

Dene on 'May the best house win'

Pier. I feel honoured to have shared these stages with some of the legends in showbiz.

My last summer season before Covid hit us was with Joey Blower, a comedy legend and good friend. I have been friends with Joey for many years as he booked us to do a summer season in Rhyll, North Wales. We had great fun and many laughs way back then, I can remember we had rehearsed a new show for the season with Joey in Rhyll. Our crew had put out the lyrics on my monitor just in case I forgot the words to the first song, 'Blow the house down!'. Joey had

seen this, unbeknown to me, and exchanged them for a sign which just said 'Fuck off!!!'.. Ha, ha, he is well known for his windups.

Joey was one of my guests when I did 'The Voice UK' for the BBC. He has been a family friend for many years now. Thanks for your continued friendship Joey Blower.

Also, I would like to thank the many friends I have made in Blackpool for their support and love including, Kristian Carter, Steve Lockheart, Kel Wood, Mick Miller, Johnny Vee, Charlotte and Tracey Dawson. Much love to you all.

Dene and Charlotte Dawson

Dene & Joey Blower

The Coffee
ICE CREAM PARLO

Joey Blower, Ian Robinson & Dene - David Green at the back

DENE MICHAEL

Chapter 16

Disaster strikes again with my disablement.

Whilst doing all these shows on TV I was suffering with sciatica and cellulitis due to my previous car accident at the age of 17. My surgeon said in years to come I would have problems with my left leg as it was severely damaged and eventually it got too bad to cope with. I was becoming very ill with the pain and having mobility problems. I think that the job we did previously running a pub restaurant in Halifax, called 'The Long Can Hall', didn't help, as I had to lift barrels of beer and keep a good cellar, which was very hard work and took it out on me. Also, having a wife that was an Alcoholic didn't help.

I met some lovely friends there - Jane and Andrew Marriott from Halifax Wedding Cars and George and Mary Sumner, who also live in Halifax, they were very helpful and gave me tips on how to run the pub as they knew most of the locals. I put on some great shows in there and many celeb' guests would come and visit, including Billy Pearce, Graham Pickles from the Mulldoons and a host of other acts that Mike supplied once again from Flair Entertainments.

After leaving the 'Long Can', I opened two other bars called 'Agadoos', with a business friend, Johnny Kerr from Sunderland and Bruce Jones (Les Battersby), my good friend of many years.

We opened one pub in Sunderland on Vine Street in the town centre and one in Batley, on what was then the Golden Mile, sadly disappeared now! It was once thriving, but we opened at the end of the good days and the crowds were disappearing, so we lost a lot of money on both of the bars, so they shut down, unfortunately.

I think it was the start of many pubs and clubs declining due to cheap booze in the supermarkets and also the smoking ban. A funny story from Agadoos, Sunderland, was when we opened on the first week we had a big plastic, full size Gorilla in the doorway, to attract peoples attention. Some drunken thug tried to steal it and ran off down the road with it, with Bruce running

Dene with his alter ego Puppet

Dene with Billy Pearce

Dene & daughter Kelli

Dene with Graham Muldoon

after him shouting 'bring it back' and the paparazzi got the picture and it made the papers next day. Good publicity for us though.

It's such a shame our Working Mens Club industry was in decline for a lot of the acts, because we all relied on these clubs and pubs for our work and wages. I was brought up in the WMCs and that's where I learnt my trade. So sad there's not many of them left now, there seems to have been so many pulled down and made into blocks of flats.

Around this time I was asked by my good friend, Liam Halewood, if I would like to do 'The Gay Pride' festivals around the country.. if I could perform on some of the shows, as Black Lace were very popular with the LGBT+ community, and had become icons, along with Kylie and Shirley Bassey (who I'd worked with earlier in my career at Batley Variety Club). I, of course, said yes. Although I'm not Gay, I have

many friends that are, and have made many new Gay friends at the concerts. After meeting these people, they are the most wonderful, loving human beings that you could ever wish to meet, and I fully support them.

After this, I worked for Leeds City Council, driving a bus taking people with special needs to school and back and also people in wheelchairs to day centres, and taking people home from hospitals. I really enjoyed this job and met some lovely people along the way. My bosses were Anthony Higgins, who became a very good friend, and Jayne Hookham, and lots, lots more including lots of the other drivers.

It was hard work, but very enjoyable and fulfilling, as lots of the clients depended on me and I felt I was making a difference in their lives.

I was getting worse day by day at this time and couldn't work, so I

Mr Agadoo

Dene with Beth Parsons

Dene with Mick McGinnley

stayed at home and was living on Disablement Benefits, as I'd lost all my money on different ventures with the clubs and bars.

It was a big change in lifestyle and I had to rent an apartment in the village where Mum and Dad Lived in Barwick in Elmet, Leeds, paid for with my Disability Benefits.. and still having to cope with an alcoholic wife, who was getting worse as well. She would hide bottles of vodka under the sink and also put it into water bottles, thinking I wouldn't know what she was up to. It was all getting too much! This was over a period of around 3 years.

I had to be strong and deal with my disability and cope with the stress of living with Karen. Adding to that, also, I didn't get any help from her family as her children didn't like me, as they felt it was my fault that their family had split up.

That wasn't the case, as Karen was very unhappy with her life before me. She had told me that the whole family was very controlling and she felt she had to get away from them, thats why she turned up on my doorstep previously.

Anyway, I was having treatment for my leg and was getting a little better, so onwards and upwards...so I thought!!! But not to be!!! Next set back, about to happen...

My first Radio presenting job was with Minster FM in York.

I was taught how to DJ and learned all the techy things a radio presenter has to do. A big thank you to David Green and Beth Parsons for showing me the ropes, as we say.

I had many happy years here doing various road shows etc. and Christmas lights switch-on's etc., and of course presenting my Saturday night party show, 'Mr Agadoos Saturday night Party.'

Dene presenting at Minster FM 104.7

minsterfm
104.7

Chapter 17

Doing time in Prison.

As I was getting a bit better, I had a call from a charity to see if I would perform for them in a Theatre in Halifax West Yorkshire, it was to raise money for under privileged children. I've always performed shows for charity all through my singing career and always there to help if I can. I explained I was now disabled and wouldn't be able to do a full show as I couldn't stand for long, so I agreed to just do 2 songs for them. Wrong move!!!!! Someone in Karens family rang up the benefits people and told them I was working. I'd also done a similar thing at a friends wedding, just a few songs, because I'd agreed to sing at their wedding a few years previously and didn't want to let them down.

It's funny how the benefits people knew I was going to sing at this private event! Wonder who told them?

Anyways, I had a letter from the benefits office asking me to go in to see them for a meeting.

They asked me what I was doing singing in a theatre in Halifax, and produced a photo of me on stage singing. They said "is this you?" I said, "of course it is" - you could see plainly it was me, due to the red glasses and hawian shirt. I told them I was singing to raise money for charity and wasn't getting paid for the appearance, they told to me it doesn't matter.. "if you can go on stage and perform for charity you can go on stage and get paid for your services".
I told them I only sang 2 songs and didn't do a full show, and I wouldn't be paid much just to do two songs anywhere else. But, they weren't giving in. They then produced a photo of me singing at my friends wedding. I wonder where they got that from, as it was a private event??? I explained, I only did a few songs, it wasn't a full gig. Again, they were not having any of it.

A few weeks later I had a letter to say I had to go to County Court about the matter, which I did, and they threw the case out and said it would have to go to Crown Court. I was very worried as my Solicitor said, "this isn't good, I think they are going to make an example of you! Not fair, but its because of your celebrity status."

So, a few weeks later, I had to go back to Crown Court, so I had a Barrister and Solicitor this time. I think the Judge had already decided I was going to jail as my Barrister phoned me the day before my court appearance to say "pack a case, you may have to go to prison." I felt awful, and very worried, as you can imagine, as I'd never been in trouble with the law all through my life.

So, the next day I went to court, there were paparazzi everywhere waiting for me and chasing me down the street outside the court with press and TV cameras everywhere. The Judge gave me a 6 month sentence in Armley Jail. They put me in cuffs and took me downstairs to a holding room in the courthouse. After I'd been checked in, my Barrister and Solicitor came to see me and they couldn't believe what they had done to me. They said if it would have been anyone else they would have got a slap on the wrist and told not to do it again, but, of course, I had to be made an example of, so others wouldn't do it. They put me in the prison van and off I went to Armley Jail.

When I arrived in Prison they put me in a cell, next to me at either side were murderers, thieves and all sorts, mainly foreign people..

I felt so out of place, even the prisoners and prison officers said to me I shouldn't be in here.

A lot of the in-mates made friends with me as they had seen me on the television in their cells on the news, so was expecting me in Armley. I made lots of friends in there and realised a lot of them shouldn't have been in there also.

I heard many stories from inmates in there. When I went for my medication I had to pass the telephones where the other prisoners would phone their families and friends. I was asked by many of them when I was passing them to speak to their wives and girlfriends on the phone and sing Agadoo to them.

I can also remember when it was lights out time all the shouting started from cell to cell and they would shout up to me as I was on the top floor in the wing (C wing) "Agga,," all the inmates used to call me "Agga".. "sing us Agadoo", which I did and most of the wing would join in. This happened most evenings!

My pad mate (cell mate) Mark, used to to go out shop lifting as he didn't have anywhere to live, he was on the streets. So in the winter he would go out and steal and let the police catch him so he would go to jail and have a warm bed and be fed 3 meals a day, have TV etc., in his cell and have smokes etc. Life sucks for some people. I felt so sorry for him.

There was lots of what they called 'Spice', a legal high, going around prison and all sorts of drugs which I kept away from, as I've never taken drugs in my life, other than for my health. It made people crazy and they would pass out and have fits. I saw it many times and it caused all sorts of problems for the Prison officers as people were walking around like zombies, when we were allowed out of our cells for exercise.

We were in lockdown for 23 hours a day due to staff shortages. The prisoners were complaining, but I didn't know any better as it was my first time inside. I saw 2 suicides whilst I was there.

I only had to do 10 weeks of my 6 months sentence as it was my first offence, and for good behaviour. Then I had to wear a tag on my ankle for 2 weeks.. what good that did, I don't know!

When I was allowed out of Prison all the inmates gave me a good send off.. they formed a conga line in the exercise yard. It felt soo.. good to be going home.

My parents and family had come to visit me as much as they could, but my wife Karen only visited me a few times whilst I was in there, which I felt was a bit strange. Anyway I was free to go home, thats when my mental health problems, anxiety and depression started again.

DENE MICHAEL

EW TO
LAS VEGAS
The Ultimate Experience !

IALS & GRAPHICS BY NATHON CHAMBERS

Chapter 18

Dealing with mental health anxiety and depression. Break up with wife number 4.

So, I was eventually back home, but things weren't good with Karen and I couldn't settle. When you're locked away in a small cell for hours on end you keep getting up and walking around your cell to stop the aches and keep your joints from seizing up, this was happening when I arrived home and she said "why do you keep getting up and walking around?"
I said "it's just something I've got into the habit of doing, while being locked away." She didn't understand!

I noticed the drinking had got even worse with her and she just wasn't the same with me. We had drifted apart and she decided to go back to Manchester to her family, it was like a weight had been lifted off my shoulders. We are now divorced and I've not heard from her or her family since.

So I was on my own again and found it really hard dealing with this depression and mental health issues. I felt so alone and wondered why it had all happened to me. I found it hard to find work again as no

4th Wife Karen

Dene, Bruce & Chris Morris at The White Star

one would employ me due to having been in Prison. If it wasn't for my parents and my children I don't know what I would have done, but luckily I had so much support from them and it really helped me to go forward. I love my family dearly and really appreciate all of them.

This walking about went on for quite a while, I didn't like going out much as I felt everyone was looking at me and talking about me. Karen had left me with our 2 dogs, Boo Boo (Agabooboo) and Ted, so I had to go out and take them for walks, so that was a good thing that came from bad, I suppose.

The dogs were so much company to me and kept me occupied looking after them. The only work I could get at this time was back in the Working Mens Clubs and Pubs, through my good friend Mike Hainsworth at Flair Entertainments. Thank you Mike for believing in me and

keeping me going, it was like starting again, all my hard work through the years had just been taken away from me.

I slowly built up my reputation again as an entertainer and would go back to do work in Spain, when times were hard here in the UK. One particular week I took Mike Hainsworth with me to meet Roland Naylor and Brian Stubbings who were in charge of bookings for the Marina Hotel. Mike did some business with him and arranged for some of his acts to go over to perform. Always nice to help if you can. I took Bruce with me again and we did an 'Audience with Bruce Jones and Dene Michael', which was very successful and we still do that show to this day. Another show we put together was 'The Lace Boys' - it was Chris Morris from Paper Lace and myself from Black Lace, hence the Lace Boys. We would perform all over the UK and again in Spain at the White Star in the

Boo Boo & Ted
Dene & Jeni Jaye

Hotel Marina complex, Benidorm. It was a great show and our voices blended perfectly and we got on very well, it was just the distance where we lived that caused a problem as Chris lived in Bodmin, Cornwall and I lived in Leeds, so it wasn't viable to do shows really.

It was at this time John wagstaff wanted me to do some Black Lace recordings so we did them with Chris in Chris Morris Studio down in Bodmin, where I had done my solo album. Also, John had an offer for us to do the 'Lets Rock the 80's' festivals, as a trial, to see how the Black Lace show would do at the festivals. So I asked Chris if he would be interested and he agreed, so we rehearsed the Black Lace songs together and went off to Bristol for a trial. We stormed it!!! We're still doing 'Lets Rock the 80's' to this day. Chris and I would carry on going to Benidorm whenever we could and Roland could fit us in. We carried on doing this for around 2 seasons and loved our time in Spain. I was starting to get out of being depressed and my mental health was a lot better, I think it was because I was a lot happier and things were returning back to normality once again.

I would also carry on going to Salou to do the reunions show for Rodney Pipor of RJP Entertainments. He was another friend who had faith in me and gave me another chance to work for him. It paid off, as every time I go there the place is packed and ther's such a good atmosphere. I go every year to perform for Rodney.. cheers pal!!! Mum and Dad would look after Boo Boo and Ted, whilst I was away in Spain - they love being at Grandma and Grandads and Mum and Dad loved them, which was great until disaster happened again, which I will tell you about in the next chapter.

Dene on the Let's Rock tour

Dene & Chris Morris

THE
LACE
BOYS

DENE MICHAEL
BLACK LACE

Chapter 19

Dealing with the death of my father.

One day around this time I had a call from Roland again to go and work in the White Star in the Marina Hotel in Benidorm to perform a solo show for them. I took up the opportunity and off I went to Benidorm. Mum and Dad looked after Boo and Ted (my two dogs) whilst I was performing in Spain. I used to phone them every night to see how things were. On the Friday of that week I had spoken to Mum and Dad and all was fine except my father Eric had been having some tests at the doctors for his heart. They had put him on Warferin tablets earlier that week to thin his blood. On the Saturday of that week Dad had taken Boo Boo out for a walk to the post office in the village to buy a newspaper. When he was outside the Post Office, Boo had seen another dog and pulled Dad over us Boo was trying to get to the other dog. His lead was caught around Dads hand and Dad fell over and hit his head and face on the pavement and was bleeding. He was on his way back home to Mum and Mum said 'you must go to Hospital that injury looks bad.'

Off they went to Hospital at St. James's (where I was born). They had to wait for 5 hours to be seen as the Hospital was very busy and had said that Dad wasn't a priority and would be seen asap. After being seen they stuck his gum with glue where it had bled. It kept

Bruce Jones, Chris Morris, Dene & Paul Taylor

bleeding due to the Warferin. They should have done a scan on his head also, due to his age (86), but did not and sent him home. They ordered a taxi for Mum and Dad to go home! As Mum took Dad to the taxi Dad still wasn't well and collapsed into Mum's arms. They took him back into the Hospital - they were gobsmacked, but it was too late he had had a stroke by the taxi. It was too late, they couldn't save him, he was choking on his saliva.

My Son Nicky phoned me just before I went on stage in Benidorm to say Dad was in a bad way and told me what had happened. I franticly tried to get a flight back to England and asked the staff and the DJ, Adam, if they could find me a flight whilst I was on stage as we had a full house of people waiting for me to appear. By the time I had finished my show Adam had sorted me a flight back, but it was to Newcastle and they wanted 800 euros for the flight one way to Newcastle, but obviously I paid it just to get back as quick as I could.

I ran upstairs to my room in the hotel and quickly packed all my clothes and stage clothes into my case. By this time it was about 4 in the morning (Sunday) and I had to get to the airport. I ordered a taxi to take me, another 100 euros more and I was at the airport. The taxi driver told me it was because it was through the night he had to charge me 100 euros for what took just over half an hour at that time!! What a rip off, but all I wanted to do was get back to Dad. I phoned my very good friend Gaz to pick me up from Newcastle airport to take me to Leeds hospital and arranged to meet him off the flight.

As I landed in Newcastle, Dad passed away, My brother Simon phoned me as I landed and told me the news, I was gutted I wasn't there for his passing. I had only spoken to him the day before and all was fine, it just shows you, you never know how

Mum & Dad

Mum & Dad

long you have on this Earth.

The next step was to arrange his funeral. He had many friends, as he was a big Crown Green Bowling fanatic and had made many friends through his bowling. And, of course, letting all our family know what had happened to Dad.

We had his funeral at the local Church in Barwick in Elmet in Leeds, it was full to the brim and people outside that couldn't get in from all over the world. My cousin, Sally Ann Brown, had come from Australia with her son Cody, for the funeral, people had travelled from Spain and all over the UK. Dave Jeffrey, my best friend, had travelled from London to be with us. My family and friends from the Midlands had also travelled up for Dads funeral, he was a very loved and popular man. Everyone loved my Dad and didn't have a bad word to say about him.

My manager, John Wagstaff, and his wife Sandra, came to Dads funeral also. John asked me if I would like to do Black Lace again with Craig Harper, another one of Mike hainsworths acts and for him to be the new member of Black Lace. I agreed and we started to do the 'Lets Rock the 80's' festivals again, which I'd previously done with Chris Morris the year before. So still 'pushing my pineapples' again.. lol.

We had a big party for Dad in celebration of his life in the local pub 'The Black Swan'. Clive, the Landlord of the pub, and his family said he'd never seen a funeral like this in the village. Dad had such a good send off with lots of singing and laughing and remembering his wonderful life.

Below is my friend Wendy King who won Opportunity Knocks singing and playing her banjo. Wendy was featured in the film 'Never mind the quality feel the width'. Since dad died I'm proud to say I've been working with her, and what a wonderful talent.

Dene and Craig Harper

Rock the 80's - Dene & Craig Harper, Black Lace

HEAVEN

Wendy King & Dene

Chapter 20

Covid strikes. More stress and family illness to deal with.

So we're all in Lockdown. This dreadful Covid has arrived and we're all stuck in our homes. All gigs have been cancelled, no money coming in, more stress!!! This has sparked my mental health issues again.. anxiety and depression to deal with once

more. Also the health of my mother is deteriorating since my father passed away. I try to be with Mum as much as I can to take her out and look after her needs, such as going shopping for her, just getting her out in the fresh air. This had become more or less impossible until we formed our 'bubble', so to speak. My brother Simon lives with Mum and does a great job looking after her, but I also want to look after Mum the best we can. I phone Mum 2 times a day to make sure she is ok.

Also, my daughter Kelli, was very ill. Kelli had the vaccine for Covid, which she had to have for work as she is a care worker, and she had a really bad reaction to it. So more worry and stress.

The only thing I could do at home was to do the Zoom interviews for charity, where I would perform in my house to various people through the wonder of Zoom.

I did one with Bongos Bingo, I'd

Dene & Mum

Dene & Mansell Stewa

just started working with them before lockdown and thankfully I now have more shows coming up with them. It's a great atmosphere at Bongos Bingo, you must go if theres one on near you.. well recommended.

I altered the words to Superman for lockdown and did a version again for charity via internet for 'Let's Rock the 80's'. It was a big success.. they made lots of money for Child Bereavment UK.

I also started writing this book, as I thought it would be ideal to use the time I was in lockdown to do this.

It's been a long hard slog for us all through this Covid situation.. I feel so sorry for people who have lost loved ones through this pandemic. We nearly lost Mum after she had her vaccine as she had a bad reaction to it and it made her have what they call a mimic stroke. She had all the symptoms of a full blown stroke, but they just

said we will keep an eye on her in hospital. So back to St. James's Hospital in Leeds, but this time we could not visit her.. a now 86 year old lady on her own in hospital is not nice. Mum is a strong lady and after a week in there she was allowed home. Whilst in hospital Mum had contracted this dreaded disease Covid. She didn't know at the time but had passed it onto myself and my brother Simon. Thanks to my bestie, Emma Barton, she looked after me whilst I had to isolate. She would cook me food and bring me groceries and leave them outside my door.. thats a true friend for you!!! Thanks Emma x. Also, a big thank you to Mansel Stewart for caring about me and my mum. Mansel has been a family friend for a long time and always gave me a call to see how I was doing. Thank's Mansel.

About a week after Mum came home she did have a bad reaction to Covid and then did have a full blown stroke so she was

Bongo Bingo Boys

Dene & Emma Barton

rushed back into hospital again, this time to the Leeds General Infirmary, ward 21. Mum was in there for about a month on her own, my brother and I would take her clean clothes etc., outside the ward, but obviously wasn't allowed in to visit. It was so frustrating to know Mum was just around the corner in the ward, but we could not see her. It was awful for Mum also, because she was so lonely without us. A massive thank you to all the doctors and nurses for looking after Mum and getting her back on the road to recovery once again.

After suffering for so long with anxiety and mental health issues I decided to get help from Victoria Carter from Leeds who is an expert in this field.

Victoria has made a big difference to me with her Rapid Transformational Therapy. I can highly recommend this for anyone with issues .

I am currently dealing with mind issues and weight issues due to the Pandemic, we're all going through lately. Since my last consultancy with RTT I have shed 5 lbs in weight and feel more relaxed with myself and more calm. I now have a goal to reach for, after speaking with Victoria, and owe a lot to her for sorting me out.

Thank you Victoria Carter you're a true pal. x

Dene with Victoria Carter

Dene with Victoria Carter

Chapter 21

Looking ahead to pushing my pineapples again.

So, looking ahead now towards my retirement and future plans. This year has been quite stressful again I've had to sell off some of my assets just to live and pay the bills with the Covid situation. I'm hoping to be able to start performing again from July this year 2021, We have not done any gigs since March, last year 2020. Myself and Craig have bookings in with Black Lace again for the 'Let's Rock the 80s' festivals, also Butlins 80's weekenders and various festivals around the UK. Hopefully, these will all go ahead.

I've been recording some new material, Country style, with my friend Paul Jackson in Sunderland. I met Paul through a mutual friend, John Kerr, who I mentioned earlier in the book. We did a version in lockdown of a song from America called 'The Get Up Dance'. We called ourselves 'Dene Michael and the Lockdown Cowboys'. It was very hard to do as we had to do it all via the internet. All the singers and dancers, Jenni Jaye, Rik Gaynor, Marc Bolton and all the dancers, had to record their bits and send it through to the production team to put it all together. It was fun though, and we're hoping that when all the Line Dancers can get back together in the clubs that they all will be doing the Line Dance to it, and it will become a big hit in the UK! Over 70 million people have viewed

Dene with Dave Fisher

Paul & Karla Hughes

the original version in America. We have a wonderful promotions lady working with us on many of the projects, called Trin Reese. Trin does a marvellous job and we all really appreciate all she does for us. Thanks Trin x.

If you have got this far without nodding off you will know that I have lead a very eventful and diverse life. As the saying goes, I believe I can genuinely say… 'Been there, done that, got the t- shirt'.

However, there is one thing that happened to me this year, and that is I met 'Steve Collins' the designer and publisher of this very book. My first introduction to Steve was when I interviewed him on my 'True Radio Show' the home of proper good music and proper good interviews.

The interview was broadcast in February this year. Now, I normally split my interviews into three sections, but this guy was so fascinating that for the first time

ever I gave him four sections on the show.

Steve is a professional designer, writer and publisher, and that in itself would be an absorbing story. However, one of the things he is probably most famous for is the work he has done over his lifetime that has literally saved the lives of thousands of people all over the world, which is an extraordinary achievement.

He delivers highly specialised training to both the private and public sectors with specific focus on weapons related crime and personal protection from violence, aggressive behaviour and terrorism.

He has become an internationally recognised speaker, and lectures to government agencies, universities and corporate bodies on officer and public safety issues, with specific focus on weapons awareness and personal protection from violent attack.

I am proud to tell you that Steve

Dene with Paul Jackson

Stay Safe Charlie & Charlotte

invited me to take part in a new training programme he is developing to teach kids about how to stay safe and if they feel frightened or threatened what they can do to protect themselves. It's not self-defence and it's definitely not martial arts. No, it's all about teaching kids awareness, and how to avoid danger.

As a father of four kids with ten grand children as soon as I heard It was all about protecting children I was onboard and thought what a fantastic project to be involved in.

Steve has invented two little characters called Stay Safe Charlie and Stay Safe Charlotte. Steve says that Charlie and Charlotte are cool dudes and 'Bully Proof Kids' because they know how to look after themselves and how to keep out of harm's way.

Steve wants me to help him with some of the presentations and do some voice over work for the lyrics of a song he has written about staying safe, for the kids to learn.

I am also working with my close friend, Paul Jackson. Paul is composing the music for Steve's song.

I am also working with another close friend, Jenna Fan, a great musician and vocalist. Jenna and I are the voices of Stay Safe Charlie and Charlotte, and together with Steve we are hoping to put a presentation together for children's television.

I am really excited about the future of this project and looking forward to the escapades of Charlie and Charlotte... as Steve would say, Stay Safe!!

I met Jenna Fan through True Radio, she was a presenter when I first started presenting my shows for them on the weekend. I'm still presenting my show on True Radio, Sundays from 7pm until 10pm every weekend with my celebrity guests. Every week I have my good friends Paul and Karla Hughes on, doing a feature with the news and the views with

Dene, Paul Jackson & Jenna Fan

Steve Collins

Keep your kids safe in this dangerous world

WITH STAY SAFE CHARLIE & CHARLOTTE

BULLY PROOF KIDS

Steve Collins of REACT Tactical Solutions has developed an educational programme to teach kids how to stay safe, and if they feel frightened or threatened, what they can do to protect themselves.

Steve has created 2 little characters...

Stay Safe Charlie and his girl friend Charlotte. Charlie and Charlotte will teach kids how to stay out of harm's way.

Dene Michael and Jenna Fan have kindly agreed to be the voices of Charlie and Charlotte on a presentation for children's TV.

junior R·E·A·C·T
THINK SAFE · ACT SAFE · STAY SAFE

Dene Michael
the voice of
Charlie

Jenna Fan
the voice of
Charlotte

the 'Hughes from America'. I met Paul previously in Spain, doing the shows at the Casino. I love doing this show it's been great having something to do through lockdown.

Another great person I am working with is Lawrence Stone who is a great business man. He has helped me tremendously to get back on track and is an inspiration to me.. thanks Lawrence, I'm looking forward to keep working with you in the future on various projects along with David King.

Brian Huggy Farmer, Ben Farmer and Lloyd Spencer, of Gaaard Protection, I would like to thank you all personally for your friendship and sponsorship in all I do.. again, its all appreciated, very much. I met these guys doing a version of 'You'll Never Walk Alone' for the Bradford Fire Disaster Fund charity record and they have become good friends and still are to this day. Looking forward to carrying on working with you At Gaaard

Protection in the future!!!

My radio show on True Radio will carry on and I'd like to thank Dave Fisher, a big fan for many years, and now also a true friend. He's never missed one of my radio shows, he's always there. Even when I worked as a presenter at Minster FM, in York, Dave never missed a show. Thanks for your friendship Dave.

Another big fan I'd like to give a mention to is Kerstin Freye, from Germany. Kerstin travels by plane to see my gigs with Black Lace and even comes to my solo shows when she can. Thank you for your support Kerstin x.

I'm very much looking forward to performing live again on stage so hope to see some of you at the gigs, don't forget to come up to me for your books signing, I'm very approachable. Look out for me on TV, I have a few enquiries from TV companies for reality shows so keep an eye out for me.

Rik Gaynor, David Thorner & Dene

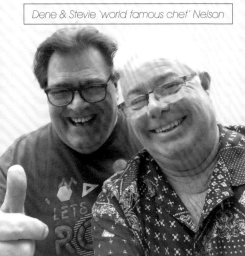
Dene & Stevie 'world famous chef' Nelson

MARC BOLTO

Thank you all for buying this book. I hope you all enjoyed learning about my life and times.

Keep safe everyone.

Here's to many more years and to pushing many more pineapples!!!

Lots of love to you all..

Dene Michael Betteridge.

By the way, if you think this is the end, think again.. there's a lot more to come!   *DM*

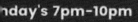

LIVE ENTERTAINMENT WITH

Dene Michael

MR AGADOO - BLACK LACE

The new album from Dene Michael 2021

HOLD ME NOW

DENE
MICHAEL
HOLD ME NOW

www.denemichael.co.uk

Available on iTunes · available on amazon music · COMPACT disc

Taken from the album Hold Me Now
as featured in the movie

THE MOVIE · WOMBLE

Dene's new album
featuring 14 fabulous new tracks
Produced by Chris Morris

1   One chance in life

2   Keeping it alive

3   Want me to be
    (baby tonight)

4   Running away

5   Hold me now

6   Start again

7   Set me free

8   I'm gonna love
    you forever

9   Then there was you

10 I'm coming home

11 I don't know anything

12 Marther

13 My little one

14 I'm Mr Agadoo

Dene Michael
Hold Me Now

1. One chance in life
2. Keeping it alive
3. Want me to be (Baby tonight)
4. Running away
5. Hold me now
6. Start again
7. Set me free
8. I'm gonna love you forever
9. Then there was you
10. I'm coming home
11. I dont know everything
12. Marther *
13. My little one
14. I'm Mr Agadoo

Recorded at Ocean Audio Studio, Bodmin Cornwall
Saxaphone Matt Woodland
Guitar, Keyboard Arrangements by Chris Morris
Backing vocalist Chris Morris, Lyndsey Rimmer,
and Michael Hope
Front Cover by Vidno Star UK
Back Cover Art Bridie May

Produced by Chris Morris

All songs written by Chris Morris and Dave Freeman,
except * written by Roy White

DENE'S PHOTO ALBUM

Billy Pearce

'Jeremy' & 'Jemimah' all grown up

Michelle Keegan

Peter Cox

Cheryl Baker

The Bluebells

Heaven 17

Edele Lynch

Ricky Hatton

kim Appleby & Midge Ure

Tony Hadley

Dr Raj

George Costigan

Thompson Twins

Owen Paul

Lewis Capaldi

Ted Robbins

Rodney Piper

Top Loader

Les McKewan

Shane Nolan

Mike Nolan

Philip Schofield

Richie Blackmore

Chesney Hawkes

Tommy Cannon

Stan Boardman

Francis Rossi

Nathan Moore, Pat Sharpe,
Dave Benson Phillips

Billy Ocean

Jason Donovan

Nick Hayward

Shane Ward

Black Lace

Andy Bell

Pat Sharpe

Keith Lemon

Marc Almond

Stephen Mulhern & Brian Conley

Stavros Flatley

Chris Moyles

Andrew 'Freddie' Flintoff

Bruce Jones

Mr Maker

Brian Farmer

Wendy King

Emma Willis & Marvin Humes

Lawrence Stone

Alistair McGowen & Ian Robinson

Sheila Ferguson

David Shapiro

Hacker & Chris

Gary Lineker

Ben Farmer

Ted Robins

Jem Frazer

Diane 'Jet' Youdale

Edward Woodward

Natasha Hamilton

Sponsor

Brian (Huggy) Farmer

GAAARDProtection
www.gaaardprotection.com

LEGEND. A word often banded about with no real foundation. Your drinking buddy comes back with the drinks from the bar and a packet of cheese and onion crisps and he's a legend. Dene on the other hand is a true legend, he's had a roller coaster of life of fame and fortune and is genuinely a lovely person and I'm honoured to call him my friend.

My name is Brian "Huggy" Farmer #goodwoodledge and real off-roader! I have a near complete Bucket List, I've also known Dene for some years now thanks to this list. One of the entries being to appear in a music video, quite how I was going to attain this was still an enigma at the time.

We all know Agadoo, If you don't then you've been living under a rock or on the moon, although the late Neil Armstrong no doubt would have pushed pineapples sometime in his life. The notion of this song is ingrained in our life, whether at a school disco, a wedding or a party anywhere, this a staple on the playlist to put a smile on the faces of the guests, some groan: but deep down they know all the words and know the dance!

My sense of humour led me to telling people I played a triangle with a local Reggae band(which I actually have done), stating: "I just stand at back and ting". This led to being invited through a mutual friend to attend a recording studio to appear on The Crowd's version of You'll Never Walk Alone for the Bradford Royal Infirmary's Burns Unit.

This is where I met Dene Michael along with Billy Pearce and The Chuckle Brothers for the first time. I tried to out humour Billy with a joke, it must have worked as Barry Chuckle gave me a "to me". I never returned it with a "to you" and keep it to this day!

My wedding approached and I believed some of the traditions were being diluted and the conga was no longer done. Who better to start this than Dene? A phone call later and he's coming along to do it live at our reception. This cemented a great friendship and a mutual appreciation for truly terrible Dad jokes, a humorous conversation turns into a competition to out gag each other.

GAAARD Protection Ltd stepped in to sponsor Dene and his new radio show on True Radio and he agreed to work with us as brand ambassador. It makes perfect sense to have the singer of Agadoo recording a parody of the million selling 1984 hit, now known as AGAAARDOO.

As GAAARD Protection's name and brand becomes global we are delighted to be on this trip with Dene. His music is known all over the world, I attended a wedding in Surat Thani province in southern Thailand, we danced with the locals to Agadoo, they knew the words.

Truly endearing are the moments spent with Dene, from being stuck in a traffic jam in his car with an allegedly broken car radio and no music other than his greatest hits CD on, to him coming to Huggy's bar to personally sing Happy Birthday to me and giving me a Gold Disc and having a good old singalong (that's why I play the triangle at the back!)

He always has an infectious smile and is great to spend time with, his dress sense however…

I was driving my Rolls Royce along the motorway when all of a sudden it wouldn't go above 30 miles an hour. So, I pulled over and rang the breakdown service. I told them the problem and they asked me what gear I was in? I said, "my wellies and donkey jacket".

The police stopped me on another day and said I was speeding! They said I was doing 50 miles an hour in a 30 miles an hour limit. I said I can't have been! I've not even been out an hour!

I bought some speaking scales the other day, I'm taking them back to the shop! I'm not being spoken to like that. I stood on them to weigh myself! They said one at a time please.

I was driving down the motorway and noticed a big lorry losing all his load, so I flashed my lights at him from behind. He wasn't taking any notice of me so I pulled up to the side of him and opened my window and shouted up to him! Your losing your load, its all coming off the back of your vehicle! He said, I'm a Gritter!

I had a black eye the other week some one said to me who's given you that black eye? I said nobody has given me it, I've had to fight for it.

I went to visit my doctors last week and my doctor said my goodness you've put some weight on during lockdown! I said I've had a lot on my plate lately.

I decided to go on holiday with a girl friend of mine a few weeks ago, we booked into what they described as a 5 star hotel! You could see 4 of the stars through the ceiling.. and I was the other one!.

We checked in to the hotel and my girlfriend said, "I don't like it here!" I said why? It's lovely! She said, "the rooms too small, mirrors everywhere, and who are all these people?" I said, "we are in the lift. "

I called into our local pet shop and I thought I would wind up the girl behind the counter. I said ive come to buy a wasp! She looked at me funny and said we don't sell wasps! I said well you had one in the window yesterday!

They said "be careful it can be 100 degrees in the shade here", I said, "it won't affect us! We are staying in the sun. "

If you think these are bad wait 'til you read the book